the Kundalini Yoga COOKBOOK

the Kundalini Yoga COOKBOOK

Feasts for family and friends

Jacqueline Koay and Ek Ong Kar Singh

The resources in this book came from KRI (Kundalini Research Institute) approved teachings and sources. The authors want to acknowledge as the main sources of reference: *Kundalini Yoga* by Shakta Kaur Khalsa; *Kundalini, the essence of yoga* by Guru Dharam Singh Khalsa and Darryl O'Keeffe; *Food for Health and Healing* by Yogi Bhajan PhD and *The Aquarian Teacher* by Yogi Bhajan PhD.

A Gaia Original

Books from Gaia celebrate the vision of Gaia, the self-sustaining living earth, and seek to help its readers live in greater personal and planetary harmony.

Editor	Camilla Davis
Design	Peggy Sadler
Production	Simone Nauerth
Photographer	Alan Marsh
Direction	Jo Godfrey Wood, Patrick Nugent

First published in the United Kingdom in 2005 by Gaia Books.

ISBN 1-85675-237-2
EAN 9 781856 752374

A catalogue record of this book is available from the British Library.

Printed and bound in China.

10 9 8 7 6 5 4 3 2 1

This book is dedicated to
the memory of Yogi Bhajan
Master of Kundalini Yoga

(26 August 1929 – 6 October 2004)

'Those who cannot see God in all cannot see God at all.'
– Yogi Bhajan

Contents

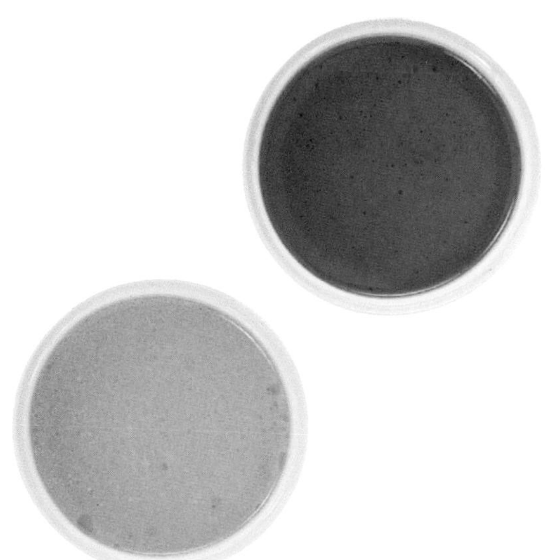

Introduction

Food for the aquarian age

'Consciousness is ecstasy; truth is our identity. We are vibrating our existence.'

Yogi Bhajan

People are often bewildered upon hearing the terminology 'yogic food' since the popular perception of yoga is tying oneself in knots and sitting for hours in meditation. How can food be yogic? You'll be surprised when we tell you that yogic food is fun, quirky, quick-to-make, sexy and delicious.

In ancient times, food was used as medicine, both in the treatment of ailments and in the prevention of illness. Unfortunately, as our modern world has 'progressed', food has become, for many of us, no more than a means of satisfying our jaded palates.

We eat foods that we know are bad for us – refined sugar, junk food, steroid-plumped meat – to stave off hunger pangs and for that sensory kick. These items often have little or no nutritional value, and at their very worst, are damaging our systems. Yet, we still go ahead and fill our bodies with unhealthy foods – all too often driven by cravings and our unhealthy relationship with food. We are living to eat, plying our bodies with detrimental foods, not eating to live. But, we are what we eat, and it is no wonder that there is so much ill health today, despite the many wonders of modern medicine. Our taste buds have become so desensitised that they have lost their ability to appreciate good food. Even when we eat 'healthy' food, we often destroy all goodness by dousing it with salt.

Yogic food uses the freshest of fruit and vegetables, organic where possible, supplemented with nuts, grains and a few store cupboard basics. The fruit, nuts and vegetables provide the *prana*, or the life force, whilst the 'heat' in the diet is provided by the dairy. However, the specific diets in this book are vegan in nature, as they were passed on by Yogi Bhajan.

The rationale behind vegetarianism in yoga is in accordance with the principle of *ahimsa*, or non-violent justice, where taking the life of another living creature can never be rationalised as a just act. Some people also believe that vegetarianism is a healthier option, because human beings have digestive systems that are similar to that of the herbivore.

We have categorised these foods, some traditional, others contemporary, under the relevant chapters. Those of you on the Kundalini Yoga path may opt to stick to either one of the three specific vegan diets included for 40 days, taking recipes and ideas from the *The Green Diet* chapter, the *Fruit, Nuts and Vegetables* chapter or the *Mung Beans and Rice Diet* chapter. Forty-day diets are part of the training when becoming a Kundalini Yoga teacher. This is because the mind works in a 40-day cycle and it requires commitment to stick to a specific regime for this length of time. Please note that it is advisable for you to consult your physician before embarking on a diet of any kind.

There are many delicious Kundalini recipes from our very rich heritage of cooking by campfires and at festivals in both Europe and America, as well as from the *gurdwaras* (places of worship) located around the world. Chapter 7, *Food to Share*, is a compilation of our favourites from the many yoga gatherings we have had the blessing to be a part of.

Food for the Chakras, Chapter 4, is a wonderful collection of ideas to help your body bring balance to these important energy centres, and to keep your mind, body and spirit functioning as a whole. The chapter entitled *Food for Women* contains recipes that are especially beneficial to women. The Kundalini Yoga principles of women's nutrition are quite simple really – prevent illness as you grow older and hang on to the positives of your youth. Stay off fizzy drinks and salt as they leach minerals from your bones; eat lots of green fruit and vegetables for cell renewal; and fill your body with wholesome foods to maintain good health. You will find a wide range of healthy, practical and delicious recipes in this chapter, all for these purposes.

For readers who merely want to enjoy a healthier diet, and perhaps absorb some of the benefits of Kundalini Yoga, this book is also written for you. The recipes from each of the chapters can be 'mixed and matched' according to what seasonal produce is available, your general wellbeing and the occasion. All recipes include insights into the Kundalini Yoga lifestyle including suggested chants and meditations, adding to the whole cooking experience.

In Kundalini Yoga, we do sets of postures and movements called 'kriyas' to cleanse our body, release energy blockages and create a sense of physical, emotional and spiritual wellbeing. These kriyas are an integral part of Kundalini Yoga, because of our wish to keep the temple of our soul healthy: this is the reason nutrition plays such an important role in Kundalini Yoga. In Chapter 9, *Yoga and Friends*, we have included several kriyas for you to share with family and friends, as well as four meditations and a number of mudras (finger positions) – also the basis for measuring out the ingredients when cooking our recipes – to help infuse the dishes with added energy and heighten both the cooking and eating experience.

Food can indeed heal, just as we can heal with our love. We all hold this ability, which we can find by opening our hearts and through touch. It is a result of the pressures of modern society and conditioning that we have lost that connection and forget this very natural ability. Even in the seemingly mundane task of food preparation, we can reconnect with the healer that exists within each and every one of us.

Therefore, an integral part of our cookbook is to prepare food with love and joy, imparting the energies of you, as the cook, into the lovingly created dishes you make. Cooking is done with feeling and a sense of being, which is why the recipes in this book use measurements that are not static and mechanical. We use pinches, scoops and handfuls – as in 'grab a handful of dried mung beans' – as our standards of measure. With touch we imbue the ingredients with our energies: this is cooking from the heart. At first, it may seem haphazard, and may even frustrate you, but once you get used to using your hands, you will discover how it can be fun, spontaneous and energising.

Perhaps most significant for us as authors of *The Kundalini Yoga Cookbook* are the words of Yogi Bhajan, father of Kundalini Yoga in the West, on the subject of food: 'Each time we eat, we are creating our future self.' It is with this spirit that we write this book.

Sat Nam

Jacqueline Koay
Ek Ong Kar Singh

SAT NAM is one of the most-used mantras in Kundalini Yoga. We say *Sat Nam* before a meal to give our thanks, or use this mantra as a closing thanks-giving at the end of a yoga class. *Sat* means Truth, and *Nam* means Identity. This is the identity of truth embodied in a primal form. Chanting *Sat Nam* awakens the soul and gives you your destiny.

The Aquarian Teacher – International Kundalini Yoga Teacher Training, Level One (KRI), 2003

Kundalini Yoga diet and lifestyle

You are what you think, do and speak

If you want to increase the benefits of your Kundalini Yoga practice, or simply improve your general health, you need to look at what you should and should not be eating. Remember, when you eat, you are creating your future self.

Food is a medicine, therefore you should eat to live – unhealthy eating will create disease. Eat well, practise your Kundalini Yoga and see God in all.

THE THREE TYPES OF FOODS

Sun Foods – all fruit, nuts, avocado and coconut
Grown more than one metre (three feet) above the ground they get maximum sun energy and are good for the nervous system.

Ground Foods – beans, rice, breads and green vegetables
Growing up to one metre (three feet) under the ground's surface, these foods contain some sun energy and some earth energy, and are great cleansers.

Earth Foods – root vegetables including potatoes, turnips, beets, garlic, ginger and onions
These vegetables grow further below the earth's surface and get the most earth energy of all foods as well as some sun energy. Earth foods contain healing properties and great energy.

THE THREE GUNAS (see p. 21)

- *Sattvic* – pure essence (most fruit and vegetables, sun foods and ground foods).
- *Rajasic* – energy to create (herbs, spices and earth foods).
- *Tamasic* – decay and negativity and should be avoided (meat, fish, eggs and fried foods; drugs and alcohol).

RAW FOOD

Very important in the yogic diet because with raw foods all vitamins and minerals remain intact.

TASTES

Just as there are three primary colours there are six primary tastes to food – sweet, sour, salty, pungent, bitter and astringent. According to Ayurveda medicine (see p. 20) all six tastes should be included in the foods we eat.

ALKALINE VERSUS ACIDIC

For optimum health, the foods we eat should have 75 percent alkalinity to help build and maintain our organs, glands and nervous system. Both sweet and sour fruit, green vegetables, pulses and legumes are high in alkalinity. Indulgences such as coffee and sweets should be avoided, as they are highly acidic.

PROTEIN

Proteins are the building blocks of your body, which is why they should be eaten regularly. Food such as legumes, nuts, seeds, beans, seaweed, rice, tofu and yoghurt are rich sources of proteins. These provide the protein that non-vegetarians get from meat.

FOOD PREPARATION AND CONSUMPTION

All meals should be prepared with love and care and should be eaten in a relaxed manner in a soothing place. Serve food with grace, pray before eating and eat consciously. Only eat when hungry, chew well and stop when you are three-quarters full. Rest after each meal and don't eat after sunset. It is also recommended you give your digestive system a rest one day a week.

FOODS AND SUBSTANCES TO AVOID

- **White sugar** – robs the body of B vitamins and creates stress.
- **Salt** – avoid over consumption as it puts pressure on the heart and inhibits absorption of calcium.
- **Nicotine** – robs the body of vitamin C and iron.
- **Refined foods** – strips the body of nutrients and B vitamins.
- **Alcohol** – addictive and poisonous to the system, placing stress on the liver.
- **Caffeine** – affects coordination, memory, perception, places stress on the heart, raises cholesterol levels, irritates the stomach and impedes or disturbs sleep patterns.

YOGIC LIFESTYLE

This, in a nutshell, is the yogic approach to food and eating. The main rules of a good yogic lifestyle are to be conscious, to cultivate moderation and to be committed to presenting yourselves before the highest awareness through meditation and study. This leads to a vital, expressive lifestyle of love, service, self-esteem and happiness. Kundalini Yoga gives access to all that already exists within your own body and mind – you just have to access it through your daily practice.

Love and respect your body,
Love and respect others,
Love and respect the Planet.

Sat Nam

1 Principles of Kundalini Yoga

Ancient technology to heal the modern world

What we eat has a huge influence not only over our physical body, the *anamaya kosha*, but also over our thoughts, and ultimately our emotional and spiritual wellbeing. The yogis of ancient times knew this, and many classical yogic texts, such as the Hatha Yoga *Pradipika*, contain advice on a yogic diet. However, proper diet is a controversial subject and it is not the aim of this book to discuss the merits of any particular diet except in relation to Kundalini Yoga and how it may benefit you.

The Kundalini Yoga approach to cooking and eating, however, is not only about what you actually eat, it is also about preparing meals with love and care, community service and helping the needy.

Infinite consciousness

To really understand the principles of Kundalini Yoga cooking, you need to understand the principles of Kundalini Yoga – a science of changing and strengthening your radiance to give you an expanded life and greater capacity. Kundalini Yoga's origins date back many thousands of years, and seem to have roots in the wisdom traditions of every culture in which a spark of consciousness had been lit.

For the early yogis, yoga was a way of life that promoted good health and spiritual wellbeing. The word 'yoga' is the derivation of the Sanskrit word '*yurg*' meaning to yoke. Yoga is therefore taken to mean a system of practice, a way of life that yokes together the mind, body and soul. By yoking together these three components, which make up the whole person, the practitioner reaches *Shuniya*, a place of peace and ecstasy. While this is the widely used definition of yoga, in Kundalini Yoga we also take the word '*yurg*' to mean the union of one's individual consciousness with the Infinite consciousness. It is a technology for awareness; of melting down the boundaries so the mind achieves its underlying infinite potential and creativeness. It is for this reason Yogi Bhajan referred to Kundalini Yoga as the owner's manual for human consciousness.

Kundalini Yoga, as taught by Yogi Bhajan, was brought to the West in 1968. The young Harbhajan Singh was born to a rich landlord family, who prayed for a male heir for 25 years. As a child he was much cherished, and at each of his birthdays he was weighed, and whatever his weight, his family would donate the equivalent weight in gold, silver and copper coins, and seven times his weight in wheat, to the poor. It is from this that the tradition of feeding the poor and the consciousness of *seva*, doing good for the community, took root in the life of Yogi Bhajan. In the Sikh *dharma* (tradition) as well as other faiths, the *langar*, or free kitchen, is where whole communities sit down to share simple foods, irrespective of gender, wealth and social status. Since Yogi Bhajan taught the Sikh *dharma* alongside Kundalini Yoga, the practice of *seva* became the cornerstone of Kundalini Yoga.

Yogi Bhajan's first experience of the West was when he arrived in Canada by invitation of a Canadian gentleman. He began teaching yoga at a popular housing facility known as Rochedale, whilst working as a clerk at a publishing house. In the December of the same year, 1968, he was invited to teach in Los Angeles by an old friend. His teachings struck a chord with the local youths, who were looking for self-knowledge, self-discovery and a way to express real and meaningful values.

Yogi Bhajan, with his students, established a 'community' in the Washington, DC area, where they set up a restaurant and a bookshop, The Golden Temple, so named after the Golden Temple in Amritsar. Reflections made by those who lived and worked at The Golden Temple during this period bears testimony to the spirit of Kundalini Yoga in the West: the familiar warmth, the sense of being part of a family and the deep spirituality it brings to one's life.

Kundalini Yoga, as taught by Yogi Bhajan, is therefore more than just a system of exercise. It is a way of life that derives its name from the 'kundalini', the energy resident in our base, or root, chakra: when the kundalini awakens, you become more conscious. With this heightened sense of awareness, you are able to reflect immediately on any actions taken, which in turn provides you with the opportunity or choice to decide what further actions you can take, or not.

For this reason Kundalini Yoga is also known as the 'yoga of awareness', and, just as all rivers end up in the ocean, all yoga results in raising the kundalini. This idea

The Golden Temple at Amritsar – the most sacred temple for Sikhs.

FIVE SUTRAS FOR THE AQUARIAN AGE

- Recognise that the other person is you.
- There is a way through every block.
- When the time is on you, start, and the pressure will be off.
- Understand through compassion or you will misunderstand the times.
- Vibrate the cosmos and the cosmos shall clear the path.

Five Sutras for the Aquarian Age according to Yogi Bhajan

is popularly depicted as a serpent coiling around a staff, representing the raising of the kundalini up the spine. In Eastern traditions, the serpent symbolises energy, essence, awareness and the play of the spirit.

The heart of Kundalini Yoga is as simple as it is beautiful – we are moving into a new age, the Aquarian Age – to a time where our lifestyles are changing our sense of space, time, relatedness and relevance. Now, at the cusp of the Aquarian Age, we are preparing to leave behind the greed and mores of the Piscean Age, for a more heart-centred world. The whole system of Kundalini Yoga prepares us for the coming of the Aquarian Age – the actions we take, the choices we make and the food we eat.

The Piscean Age was all about machineries and hierarchies; atom bombs and sexual exploitations; power and corruption. Living became a matter of survival rather than a source of joy. There was minimal beauty of the soul and little spirituality in the heart.

The advent of the Aquarian Age is moving us all to greater heartfelt awareness. With beauty in your soul and spirituality in your heart, you touch on the Infinite. Kundalini awakens you to your original Self, where you cease to be a finite being of limited potential and become a being of infinite potential. As you practise Kundalini Yoga, you are steadily growing into your expanded identity, which is the natural unfolding of your true nature.

Alongside kriyas (yoga sets) and meditation, chanting forms an important part of our daily practice. The entire Universe was built on sound, on vibration. By chanting, or vibrating, a specific sequence of sounds, you are tuning in to higher levels of consciousness. The chanting of mantras, whether silently in your heart or out loud, has the effect of guiding your mind.

When chanting, the movement of your tongue stimulates the meridian points along the upper palate of your mouth. These meridian points can be likened to the keyboard of a master computer, and are connected to the hypothalamus area of your brain. The hypothalamus is known to regulate vital functions as well as trigger the regulation of moods, emotional behaviour and sexuality. The pulses that it receives as we chant are translated into chemical signals that go to the vital areas of both our brain and our body.

Spiritually, the interaction of the tongue with the meridian points creates the experience of merging with the Divine. By chanting mantras during food preparation you are incorporating the sound of your chanting into the food. Sound is a form of energy that has structure, power and definite effects on both the chakras (energy centres) and the human psyche – this is why certain music lifts our souls. The *prana*, or life force, from the power of sound is tremendously powerful.

Kundalini Yoga is about the way you live, and since your body is your soul's vehicle in this life, keeping it healthy and clean forms an important part of a yogi's lifestyle. Because we need to eat to live, the whole subject of food, from chanting when cooking and eating, to history, to heritage and to science, becomes part of the Kundalini Yoga path.

Since, when we eat we are creating our future selves, food is an important aspect of this path: the proteins, vitamins and minerals in the food are incorporated into our structural skeleton. They are made into the blood that flows around the body and give birth to new cells that make up the physical body.

Mastery over our physical body is the first step in the journey of life for each of us. Like all vehicles, it is a complex network of working parts: such as the circulatory system, glands, brain and nervous system that easily rival the most sophisticated technology man could ever create. And this complex system needs maintenance as well as careful assessment of its capacity to act, its potential to respond to demands and its possibility for endurance and longevity.

Yogi Bhajan placed great emphasis on 'balance', including not over-eating. Like all addictions, over-eating can destroy the balance of an individual's whole system including the way we think, blocking goals and aspirations. Therefore in Kundalini Yoga there are many different 40-day diets to help break the cycle of the mind (one cycle is 40 days). These require great discipline to follow.

The mind guides your outlook, emotions and actions – it is your roadmap in this life. If you believe life is miserable, even the lightest shower of rain can prevent you from enjoying your day. However, if you embrace each day with a positive outlook you will dance in the rain – all your experiences are coloured by the creativity and appraisal of your mind. So, if you approach Kundalini Yoga with an open mind, you receive more benefit than if you start out having already decided it is not going to work for you. Experience, then believe. But we must remain open to all new experiences. Not only when it comes when following the Kundalini Yoga path but also in all other aspects of your life.

Finally, with the mind and body comes the soul, the spirit. No life can exist without a thread linking it to the spirit within this life. The definition of the spirit in yoga and the main religions is the same one God, one reality. Our origins as human beings are that we are, first and foremost, people of spirit and faith. It is only through changes in society, shifts in perception, urbanisation and a loosening of familial times that we have lost the thread. Growth with Kundalini Yoga means elevating yourself and creating a group consciousness by joining others in the practice of raising awareness.

Because food is one of the basic human needs, we, as authors of this book and yogis, believe that you can open this ancient technology, including raising consciousness, to people through food prepared and cooked according to the Kundalini Yoga tradition.This book is about evolving a healthier, holier and happier lifestyle through the key aspects of Kundalini Yoga.

May you live a gentle, joyous and blessed life.

Sat Nam

Growth with Kundalini Yoga means elevating yourself and creating a group consciousness by joining others in the practice of raising awareness.

2 The yogic staples

Positive and energetic eating

The difference between this Kundalini Yoga cookbook and other yogic cookbooks is that here we are propagating a kundalini approach to cooking. We use the trinity roots – onions, ginger and garlic. Traditionally, these are viewed as rajasic, or hot, encouraging burning passion, intense emotions and a restless spirit and therefore are not encouraged in yogic recipes. But we use them in Kundalini Yoga cooking because of their fire element as well as the grounding energy they contain. The popular use of these roots in Kundalini Yoga recipes is also because they fit into the concept of household yoga and lifestyle, as espoused by Yogi Bhajan, who recognised that modern yogis should be householders and not hermits living in remote caves; that as part of the living in the real world, we should lead normal lives. To do this food has to be tasty.

The philosophy

Here are the six basic elements of yogic food:

- Avoid food that has a mother – including meat, fish and eggs.
- Eat food that is low in saturated fats – no meat and full-fat cheese.
- Eat food high in complex carbohydrates – we need carbohydrates, but say no to food high in refined carbohydrates.
- Low salt content is important – salt leaches calcium from the bones. In yogic teaching, no added salt for women of any age and for men over 35 years.
- Consume dairy produce – for protein and its 'fire' element.
- Always prepare food with love and care.

The main element is, of course, no meat. It is believed that when an animal is killed, its fear is incorporated into its flesh. So, by eating meat, we are taking into our body all the violence and fear associated with its killing. On a scientific basis, meat contains animal proteins that undergo putrefaction a decomposing process that begins at death. Putrefaction releases toxic by-products that are absorbed by the liver, putting a strain on the system. Vegetables, on the other hand, do not undergo this form of decomposition.

Meat also produces acid, is high in cholesterol and, more worryingly, factory-farmed animals are often fed with hormones and antibiotics. These remain in their system and are incorporated into the bodies of those who eat their flesh. However, one of the most important aspects of the yoga path is non-judgment, so don't feel compelled to give up meat due to external pressures. If you follow the yogic path, then the principles of *ahimsa* – non-violence – will preclude killing animals for food. If you practise yoga as part of a training programme, then any modifications in your diet are probably related strictly to health.

However, there is more to healthy eating than staying off meat and processed, high cholesterol and salty foods. In fact, a meatless diet can be detrimental if you neglect to eat enough protein, or if you still fill yourself up with empty, refined but meat-free foods – items such as white bread and biscuits.

In Ayurveda, the science of healing that originated in India thousands of years ago, there are six tastes. According to Ayurvedic principles, for a balanced diet we should include all six tastes, in appropriate quantities. Each of these six tastes has specific actions on the three vital energies, or *doshas* – *Vata*, *Pitta* and *Kapha* – that control our psychological and physical processes. Once ingested and digested, tastes do not disappear from the food, and continue to influence our physical and emotional balance. The six tastes are sweet, sour, salty, pungent (hot), bitter and astringent. Each of the tastes is made up of a combination of two of the five natural elements – air, earth, ether, fire and water.

There are many textbooks on Ayurveda and food-combining, but in this chapter, let us just look at one example of how a particular food's elements can have an effect on the body.

Fruit, for example, are rich in the air element: they grow on trees or bushes, swing in the air and dance in the breeze. Eating too much fruit will create a large volume of 'air' in the intestines, and this can manifest itself as pain in other parts of the body. In some Eastern

Ayurveda is made up of two Sanskrit words – *Ayu* meaning life and *Veda* meaning the knowledge of. To know about life is Ayurveda.

cultures, a woman at a vulnerable stage in her life, for example immediately after childbirth, is forbidden to eat food that contains too much air, and is encouraged instead to eat warming foods such as sesame oil and fresh root ginger.

The food that we eat, as with everything else in the Universe, is governed by three primary forces, the so-called *gunas*. Unlike modern scientists, yogis are not interested in the chemical composition of the food. Instead they classify food by the three *gunas* according to its effect on the body and mind:

- *Sattva* – the quality of love, light and life.
- *Raja* – the quality of activity and passion.
- *Tamas* –the quality of darkness and inertia.

Each food type has its own signature *guna*. Sattvic food is food that is fresh, pure and unprocessed such as fresh fruit and vegetables, which are just ripe and grown without any chemical fertilisers.

Mushrooms, on the other hand, grow in the dark, feed on decaying matter and therefore adopt the tamasic qualities. Having too much tamas will make a person feel lethargic, heavy and devoid of energy.

Onions and chillies are very hot and are therefore rajasic. It is thought that over-consumption of rajasic foods will incite a person, fan the flames and arouse strong feelings. It is for this reason that widows in India are traditionally discouraged from eating hot dishes.

In Kundalini Yoga, unlike other yoga paths, we believe in the potency of the trinity roots, as already discussed. When asked about a potent life Yogi Bhajan said, 'The three roots – garlic, onion and ginger – will maintain you through the times and through the age.' We use this potent trio frequently in our cooking.

The nature of food, however, can change and cooking is the most obvious catalyst. For example, grains become sattvic, energetic, after cooking, and honey becomes tamasic, poisonous, with cooking. The nature of food can also change when combined with other foods and spices, or if it is stored for long periods. Generally grains should be aged slightly to become more sattvic, but fruit shouldn't be aged because they rot and become tamasic. Therefore, apart from cooking with lots of fresh, preferably organic, vegetables and fruit, make sure you do not spoil their quality with over-cooking or by adding a lot of additives.

Cook from the heart and infuse the food you make with love and *prana*. This is the first rule of Kundalini Yoga cooking and an important tenet of this book. Your body is the temple of your soul, and *prana* is the life force, the intangible energy that permeates every atom of the Universe. According to Yogi Bhajan, 'Our tie between us and God is the ray of light called *prana*.'

If you feel tired and fatigued for no apparent reason, it could well be that the food you eat requires more *prana* to digest it than it releases, with the net effect of expending a lot of energy, sapping your body's stores. By using fresh, easily digested ingredients, you are ensuring your body harvests maximum *prana* from it.

In the Sikh *dharma*, and subsequently in the Kundalini Yoga, the *langar*, or free kitchen, forms an important part of the yogic tradition. Men and women get together to prepare community meals, expressing their love and devotion in the food they prepare as they chop vegetables, knead chapattis and stir curries. Food cooked with devotion and love tastes wonderful, not because of costly ingredients and painstaking preparation, but because it is the embodiment of light, of good energies and intentions, and of mantras. Cook with your heart and you will notice a difference in how food tastes.

And this is how we will teach you to cook, with your fingers and your hands; with your senses and with Kundalini Yoga's guiding principles. Instead of using measuring jugs, spoons and the kitchen scales, we urge you to cook using your intuition. Feel the ingredients, smell them and go with your senses, trusting your intuition, instead of following a set of rigid instructions. Creativity is part of Kundalini Yoga – it is a personal sensory process, where you look within yourself for fulfilment.

Cooking with your heart and hands

The beauty of cooking with your heart and hands is that the food tastes slightly different each time. This in itself is an important yogic philosophy, namely not to be too attached to the outcome or results. Like life, cooking is about the journey, not the destination. Being too attached to the outcome is a limitation to self-growth. So our approach to kundalini cooking is the same as our approach to life – namely laugh, love, be in the moment and accept what comes to you as the grace of God.

As it does when practising Kundalini Yoga, chanting features strongly in this cookbook. Many of the recipes come with suggested mantras to be chanted whilst preparing and cooking the dishes. Mantra is the 'science' of sound, where the sequencing of specific words invoke positive energies. If we chant as we cook, we imbue the food with these energies and projections of the mind, which we then incorporate into our bodies as we eat the food. This is very powerful.

We also believe in every person's inherent ability to heal with touch, and this is why we invite you to cook using your hands at every opportunity. If you are not accustomed to cooking with your hands, and cooking intuitively, we have included as a guide a measurement table that covers the equivalent metric and imperial weights and volumes for the main ingredients used in our recipes. This will help you to build your confidence. However, we hope it will not be too long before you become more self-assured and adventurous, and you have no need for, or desire to use, this reference.

As well as measuring ingredients using your hands, our recipes include suggested ways to stir and very

ENERGETIC COOKING TECHNIQUES

In many of the recipes we specify the number of times to stir the ingredients or minutes to simmer a dish. This is because there are certain numbers considered powerful in Kundalini Yoga. We also suggest movements to use when stirring, pouring and sprinkling, and shapes to create when cutting and chopping. All these aspects of kundalini cooking add to the creative experience.

Numbers

Three: the number of the positive mind; the total number of *gunas*; and the number of levels of our being – emotional/mental, physical and spiritual (mind, body and spirit).
Eleven: this represents the One, the Creator and the Creation. It is connected to spiritual wisdom and is also the outcome when all the ten bodies – made up of physical, mental and energy bodies – are combined to make one.
Twenty-two: in meditation, the number 22 combines the negative, the positive and the neutral minds, so that they become one, representing balance and harmony.
Thirty-one: in meditation the number 31 affects all the cells and rhythms of the body; in cooking it affects the elements. This number also affects the mind's projection – three plus one gives four, the number for the meditative mind.
Sixty-two: six plus two gives eight and eight is the number that represents healing. It also represents the Infinite.

Movements

Infinity motion: the figure-of-eight embodies the moving beyond time and place, and the number eight, which relates to heart-centred practices and the planet Saturn.
Circle: a circle completes a cycle and it is a vortex of energy from the foundation to the Infinite. It also represents the cycle *Saa Taa Naa Maa* (birth, life, death and rebirth).
Triangle: our body is the union of two triangles – the lower triangle (first, second and third chakras) and the higher triangle (fifth, sixth and seventh chakras).

specific mixing and cooking times. Whilst this may seem strange, there are very good reasons for our guidelines. For example, when stirring, we may ask that you stir, 'tracing the outline of the infinity symbol', which means you draw a figure-of-eight. The reason for this is that the number eight relates to heart-centred practices and the planet Saturn. Saturn represents the taskmaster, the law of karma, the taking of responsibility and the courage to hold to duty.

THE MEASUREMENTS

Locking the fingers of the hands in certain positions creates pathways that guide energy flow and reflexes to your brain – it is your way of communicating to your mind and body using your fingers. It is also the reason why cooking with your hands is very beneficial.

Single handful refers to single cupped hands made by placing one hand on top of the other.
Double handful refers to the cup you make with both hands. This is done by placing your hands together, with the fingers slightly overlapping. A double handful also forms the *Gurprasaad Mudra* (see p. 140). When measuring liquids, ask a family member or friend to pour the liquid into your cupped hands and you will experience the sensual and vibrant feeling of liquid running onto your fingers. If you are cooking on your own, simply use your cupped hands to scoop up the liquid or dry ingredients.
Small gyan pinch refers to picking up a morsel between your thumb and first finger. This is also the *Gyan Mudra* (see p. 140). We use this mudra a lot when cooking, as it is a way to infuse the food (and the cook) with calming energies.
Mudra (large) pinch, refers to the amount you pick up when you join the tips of all the fingers and thumb together in the *Praying Mantis Mudra* (see p. 140). This mudra focuses and blends all the five natural elements – earth, ether, water, fire and air.
Sprinkle is when you pick spices up between your thumb and the little finger. It is used a lot when seasoning just before serving the meal. This forms the *Buddhi Mudra* (see p. 140).

Sprinkle	use your thumb and little finger
Small gyan pinch	use your thumb and first finger
Mudra pinch	use your thumb and all fingers
Single handful	a single cupped hand
Double handful	two hands held together

You can interchange the mudras used as you cook, based on the ingredient being measured, your intuition and on the food and the level of spiciness you prefer. Other options when sprinkling ingredients are the *Shuni Mudra*, which uses the tips of the thumb and third finger, and the *Surya Mudra*, which uses the tips of the thumb and fourth finger (see p. 140).

For an enhanced eating experience, you can also use these mudras to pick up the food as you eat.

MEASURING THE KUNDALINI WAY

We encourage you to cook using your hands, wherever possible, and our recipes ask you to measure ingredients using handfuls, mudra or large pinches, small gyan pinches and sprinkles (see also p. 23). The list below provides you with equivalent measures for the most common ingredients used in our recipes. These have been rounded up or down. Multiply or divide according to whether single or double handfuls are required, but remember, this is only a guide. Hopefully you will quickly become confident in your own intuition and only want to measure with your hands, being creative, and adjusting recipes to your own taste.

1 small gyan pinch	½ teaspoon
1 mudra pinch	1 teaspoon
3 mudra pinches	1 tablespoon
Aduki beans	2 handfuls/½ cup/80 g/2¾ oz
Amaranth	2 handfuls/½ cup/100 g/3½ oz
Basmati rice	2 handfuls/½ cup/90 g/3 oz
Black eye beans	2 handfuls/½ cup/85 g/3 oz
Buckwheat	2 handfuls/½ cup/100 g/3½ oz
Bulghur wheat	2 handfuls/½ cup /100 g/3½ oz
Carob powder	2 handfuls/½ cup/80 g/2¾ oz
Chickpeas – raw	2 handfuls/½ cup/125 g/4¼ oz
Coconut milk	2 double handfuls/1 cup/250 ml/8 fl oz
Desiccated coconut	2 handfuls/½ cup/75 g/2¾ oz
Flax seeds	2 handfuls/½ cup/50 g/1¾ oz
Ghee	1 handful/¼ cup/60 g/2 oz
Healing water	2 double handfuls/1 cup/250 ml/8 fl oz
Lentils	2 handfuls/½ cup/100 g/3½ oz
Milk	1 double handful/½ cup/125 ml/4 fl oz
Millet	2 handfuls/½ cup/80g/2¾ oz
Mung beans – raw	2 handfuls/½ cup/100 g/3½ oz
Mung beans – sprouted	2 handfuls/½ cup /80 g/2¾ oz
Nuts – mixed	2 handfuls/½ cup/60 g/2 oz
Oils – olive, canola	1 double handful/½ cup /125 ml/4 fl oz
Polenta/cornmeal	2 handfuls/½ cup /120 g/4 oz
Pumpkin seeds	1 handful/¼ cup/35 g/2¼ oz
Quinoa	2 handfuls/½ cup /90 g/3 oz
Rice flour	1 handful/¼ cup/40 g/1⅓ oz
Sesame seeds	1 handful/⅛ cup/15 g/4½ oz
Soya beans	2 handfuls/½ cup /80 g/2¾ oz
Soya and Rice milk	2 double handfuls/1 cup/250 ml/8 fl oz
Stock	2 double handfuls/1 cup/250 ml/8 fl oz
Sunflower seeds	1 handful/¼ cup/40 g/1⅓ oz
Tahini paste	2 handfuls/½ cup/135 g/4¾ oz
Tofu – small block	180 g/6⅓ oz
Tofu – large block	450 g/1 lb
Wholewheat flour	2 handfuls/½ cup/120 g/4 oz

RECOMMENDED FOODS TO EAT

- Fresh, sweet fruit of all types, preferably used freshly cut from the whole
- Whole grains, such as rice, quinoa, wheat and oats
- Beans like mung, adzuki and soya
- Raw nuts and seeds, such as almonds, cashews, walnuts, pecans; sunflower, pumpkin and sesame seeds
- Natural sugars such as jaggery (unrefined sugar), honey, maple syrup and molasses
- Herbs and spices, including basil, cardamom, cinnamon, coriander, cumin, fennel, garam masala, ginger, mint and turmeric
- Herbal teas, natural water and fresh juices, particularly of the citrus kind
- Foods prepared with love and consciousness

RECOMMENDED FOODS AND SUBSTANCES TO AVOID

- Meat, fish and eggs
- Artificial, processed and junk foods
- Canned food, except naturally canned fruit and tomatoes
- Animal fats, margarine and poor-quality oils
- Factory-farmed dairy products
- Fried food
- Refined foods such as white sugar and white flour
- Artificial sweeteners
- Old, stale, over-heated and reheated food
- Alcohol, tobacco and all other stimulants
- Tap water and artificial beverages
- Microwaved and irradiated food
- Genetically engineered food
- Foods eaten in a disturbed environment or eaten too quickly

SCALING UP FOR FRIENDS

Food is for sharing and this forms a large part of the Kundalini Yoga culture. Generally, a single handful of rice, mung beans or pulses is suitable for two to four people, depending on what else goes into the pot. A double handful of vegetables, or two single handfuls, is generally ample for four people, but let yourself be guided by your cooking experiences and your inner wisdom. Let the light guide you whilst you cook, and all will be tasty and healthy.

The recipes in this book, unless otherwise stated, are for four persons, so halve or multiply as you wish.

The staple recipes

In our recipes, we include certain store cupboard 'specialities' including healing water, yogic tea, traditional and instant, and yogic spices. These handmade recipes provide added flavour and energy to the food you cook and the meals you eat.

Healing water

You will need
mineral, spring or filtered water
1 large glass jar

Water is one of the most energy-sensitive substances you will use in cooking, and the power of the mantra, and our own projection whilst meditating, has a positive effect on the water within our own bodies. Healing water, as suggested in all our recipes, is created through chanting and meditation and is very energetically powerful.

The recipe we recommend is one Ek Ong Kar, the author, has been using for years and involves a very simple process. There is always a glass jar of this healing water in his kitchen, which he uses for both cooking and drinking, as well as a remedy for people who are having trouble meditating, for children and for those in search of a little peace.

- Fill a large glass jar with water, then prepare the affirmations. The suggested mantra affirmations are as follows, but you can always use your own.
- Write the mantras on little stickers and stick them on the jar, or write directly on the glass jar with a waterproof marker pen.

Love, Light, Peace
Cosmic, Infinite, God
Healthy, Happy, Holy
Sa Ta Na Ma
Ra Ma Da Sa
Sa Say So Hung
Harmony, Balance, Alignment

- Place the jar near you while meditating. When you finish hold it between your hands to transfer the powerful healing *prana* from your hands to the water.
- Each time you add new water to the jar, mix the water by making a loose fist with one hand, and with the index finger of the other hand, stir the water in a clockwise motion to create a vortex in the centre. Chant the mantra affirmations in monotone three times each.
- To enhance a particular chakra, add an appropriately coloured sticker to the jar, and then remove it when you no longer need to work on that chakra. The water will now contain all colours in pure balance – a pure white that is the amalgamation of all colours.
- We recommend using healing water in your cooking; however, when preparing our recipes you can always use mineral, spring or filtered water instead.

Sat Nam

Yogi tea

You will need
10 double handfuls healing water
8 slices fresh ginger root, finely diced
12 cloves
16 green cardamom pods, cracked
16 black peppercorns
2 cinnamon sticks
4 black tea teabags
1 double handful milk or soya milk (optional)
honey to taste (optional)

Note: 2 double handfuls liquid equals 250 ml, 8 fl oz and 1 cup

Yogi tea is good for your blood, colon, nervous system and bones, and because of the fresh ginger and spices used, it is also good for head colds, the flu and for warming and detoxing your body. This Yogi Tea recipe is the original Yogi Bhajan recipe – it is a delicious, potent, feel-good drink.

- In a saucepan bring the water to the boil, then add the spices. Cover and simmer the spiced liquid for 15–20 minutes.
- Remove from the heat, add the teabags, and let them steep in the spiced liquid for 1–2 minutes. Add the milk and honey, if using, and bring back to the boil. Remove from the heat immediately.
- Strain off the spices and serve.

Sat Nam

Instant yogi tea

You will need
1 handful cinnamon powder
1 finger-length nub fresh ginger root, grated
1 mudra pinch ground cardamom
1 small gyan pinch ground cloves
1 small gyan pinch ground black pepper

Making Yogi Tea the traditional way is great fun, however, it takes time. This version, which is made by dissolving powdered ground spices, gives you instant yogi tea that can be more convenient to make when you just want a cup for yourself and friends. This quick method means it is always available.

- Mix together the powdered spices and place them in a glass container with a tight lid. Store in a cool place.
- To make a cup of yogi tea use the powdered spices like instant coffee. Add one teaspoon to boiling healing water. You may also, if you wish, add honey as a sweetener and milk or soya milk. Mix well and strain as you would when making freshly ground coffee. Feel the happiness, health and holiness in each cup you drink.

Sat Nam

Yogic stock cubes

You will need
healing water (see p. 25)
5 large onions, diced
5 cloves garlic, minced
1 finger-sized nub fresh ginger root, grated
5 carrots, peeled and chopped
3 large tomatoes
4 celery stalks
1 parsnip
1 parsley root
1 handful fresh parsley, chopped
1 bay leaf
1 mudra pinch dry parsley
1 mudra pinch celery powder
1 square piece (thumb-nail sized) kombu seaweed
grated zest of 1 lemon
3 peppercorns
1 small gyan pinch sea salt

We love this organic yogic vegetable stock, which we make with healing water and use instead of mass-produced dried stock cubes. Once the stock is cooked, cool it down, then pour it into a ice cube trays. Place in the freezer and store until needed. Use 1 or 2 cubes when cooking, or as indicated in the recipe.

- In a large pot, add 30 double handfuls (6 litres/12 pints) of healing water plus all of the ingredients.
- Bring to the boil, reduce the heat, then simmer over a low heat for 31 minutes. Let the stock cool before placing it into a food processor. Blend with a smile until smooth. Strain and pour into ice cube trays. Freeze and use within 80 days.

Sat Nam

Yogic spice

You will need
1 handful ground cumin
1 handful ground coriander
1 handful ground ginger
1 handful black pepper corns
1 handful ground cardamom
1 handful turmeric
½ handful cinnamon
½ handful clove powder
3 mudra pinches crushed or powdered bay leaves

This is a wonderful alternative to garam masala and is used a lot in yogic and Indian cooking. The yogic spice gives every dish a distinct flavour, whilst the grounding nature of the spices enhances your stamina and promotes good health.

- Mix all the ingredients in a glass jar and keep it sealed in a cool, dark place. Use as needed.

Sat Nam

ABOVE Green chilli and lentil soup (see p. 34)
BELOW Holy spinach and herb salad (see p. 34)

3 The green diet

Cell renewal and a burst of energy

The Green Diet was given to Kundalini Yogis by Yogi Bhajan for the purpose of cleansing the body, filling it with food that is fresh, pure and unprocesssed. Of all the vegetables, green vegetables provide the richest source of *prana* (life force) as well as valuable nutrients. These are the 'super foods' that provide a tremendous boost of energy when you concentrate your diet on them.

When following this diet you are allowed to eat any combination of food, the only requirement is that whatever you eat must be green – the deeper the colour, the more nutritious it will be. This is due to the higher level of beneficial vitamins and minerals, in particular vitamin A, phyto-chemicals and carotenoids. To give The Green Diet an additional kick of energy, the recipes in this section are prepared either raw or involve minimal cooking. This ensures that ingredients remain rich in enzymes and oxygen, which get depleted through cooking.

Since it is important to get your body's daily requirement of amino acids (protein building blocks), minerals and vitamins, you should incorporate as many different varieties of 'greens' as possible. Lettuce? Cucumber? No! Whilst these are good for you, and we're not saying don't eat them, we simply want to open your mind to other realms and introduce to you other exciting 'greens' that will make you absolutely love this diet. Be prepared, though. After a few days on this diet, your stools will have a green tinge – if you are otherwise healthy, don't worry, but remember you should consult your physician before embarking on any diet regime.

Whilst on this diet we recommend you drink green tea. It contains a potent antioxidant known as polyphenol that has been linked to having anti-cancer and anti-heart disease benefits.

Whilst on the subject of drinks, let us not forget juicing. Juicing vegetables is an easy way to get plenty of 'greens' into you, and it's fun. We have included just one juice recipe, because we believe juicing is a great way to express your creativity. So start juicing. Try adding spirulina and chlorella, which can be obtained in dried powdered form, to your juices. They are a wonderful accompaniment to the Green Diet as they are easily absorbed into the system, are full of healing properties and are loaded with nutrients.

Stick to the Green Diet for 40 days and be prepared for a BIG change in your energy levels. If you are just interested in improving your diet generally, you will reap the benefits by simply incorporating more dark, green-coloured fruit and veg into your daily diet.

KUNDALINI YOGA AND THE GREEN DIET

'All that exists in the three heavens rests in the control of prana. As a mother her children, oh prana, protect us and give us splendour and wisdom.'
Prashna Upanishad II.13

The Green Diet is all about *prana*, or life force, and Kundalini Yoga is specifically about working with and harnessing *prana*. It is the life force, the first unit of energy, and it is that which keeps our bodies alive and healthy. Without *prana* the physical body is no more than a lump of clay. One of the key sources is food, and the richest source comes from those foods that are pure, not over-cooked and not over-processed. And meat? Meat requires more energy to digest, resulting in a net *prana* of nil – or even in the minus region.

A diet consisting wholly of green fruit and veg infuses the body with this life force, cleanses us and lifts the soul. Complement your Green Diet with regular practice of *asana* and *pranayama*, and even more *prana* will be taken in and stored in your body, bringing about even greater vitality and strength.

Green is also the colour of the heart chakra. So, as your body becomes more vibrant, open your heart to love, compassion, trust and acceptance.

EXPERIENCING THE PRANA

Kundalini Yoga is often associated with the image of a coiled serpent, though the meaning of the word kundalini is actually 'the curl of the lock of hair of the beloved'. It is a poetic way of describing the flow of energy and consciousness that already exist within each one of us.

Prana is the life force and *apana* is the eliminating force. When these two opposing forces are joined with Kundalini Technology, an age-old yet ultra-modern system of yoga, we create a pressure that raises the kundalini energy resident at the very base of the spine. The journey of the kundalini through the *sushumna*, or the central nerve, to the higher chakras, brings about oneness of the soul with its surroundings.

To experience a surge of *prana*, sit comfortably with your back straight, listen to your breath and meditate quietly whilst practising pulling in your *Root Lock*. To do this you first isolate your navel centre that is located three finger-widths below your belly button. Then tighten your anal sphincter, pulling it upwards and inwards towards your navel centre. Now also contract the area around your sex organs up towards your navel centre. Finally, pull your lower abdominal muscles down to this point. This is the *Root Lock*.

Now, inhale the *prana* deep down into your navel centre and pull the *apana* up with the *Root Lock* to the navel centre. This facilitates the mixing of both the life force and the eliminating force.

Next do the *Breath of Fire*, which is done in the sitting position with the spine straight. The focus is equally on the inhale and the exhale, where the breath is powerfully drawn in and expelled through the nose only: as you exhale pull in your navel, moving both your upper abdomen and diaphragm. This is done in one continuous breath with a relaxed face and body. Begin slowly, then as you get used to the rhythm, attempt two or three powerful breaths per second. Start practising *Breath of Fire* for 30 seconds – advanced practitioners may go up to 11 minutes. Avoid practising the *Breath of Fire* when menstruating or pregnant, unless it has been a strong part of your practise for a while. In this case, it may be practised, but keep the navel movement light.

Vand chakna guacamole

You will need
2 large avocados, diced
¼ green onion, diced
2 handfuls fresh parsley, chopped
1 small green chilli, finely diced
1 large green tomato, diced
juice of 2 limes (adjust to taste)
2 large green (bell) peppers
green olives (for garnish)
mixed fresh herbs (for garnish)
selection of crudité (optional)

Store cupboard ingredients
green olive oil

Vand chakna means to sit together and eat and is one of the tenets of the *dharma*, the spiritual path. According to Yogi Bhajan, in the Sikh way of life if there is no *langar*, a communal kitchen, there is no *gurdwara*, place of worship.

Sharing forms a large part of what we do, and this dish is one made for sharing. Sharing and nurturing is practical spirituality and guacamole is great for this – you can pass the dish around and everyone dunks in the crudités.

- Using a food processor, mash up the avocado with 2 single handfuls of olive oil until fluffy.
- Add the remaining ingredients and continue to blend until smooth. You may wish to add more chillies if you like your guacamole spicy.
- Remove the tops from the peppers and de-seed. Fill with the guacamole.
- Garnish with a sprinkling of seeded and sliced green olives and chopped mixed herbs. Serve with a selection of crudités or pitta bread.

Sat Nam

Broccamole

You will need
2 double handfuls broccoli stems
1 small green chilli, finely sliced
juice of 1 lime
1 garlic clove, crushed
1 small green tomato, diced
3 spring onions (scallions), thinly sliced

Store cupboard ingredients
dried cumin

The Aztec word for the avocado fruit was *ahuacatl*, which means testicle. In the past, the avocado had a reputation for inducing sexual prowess and consequently wasn't purchased or consumed by any person wishing to protect their reputation from slander. So, if you would like to make a less risqué version of the guacamole (and also one with less fat), try the broccamole instead. Broccoli is a rich source of vitamin C, vitamin A and minerals. It also provides dietary fibre and protein – so broccamole is an all-round, healthy fast food.

- Steam the broccoli stems until al dente then carefully peel off any tough outer layers.
- In a food processor purée the broccoli stems with the chilli, lime juice, garlic and 1 mudra pinch of dried cumin, until completely smooth.
- Spoon the mixture into a glass bowl and fold through the diced tomato and sliced spring onions.
- Chill before serving with a selection of green crudités.

Sat Nam

Base chakra stew

You will need
2 double handfuls mung beans
1 large green (bell) pepper, diced
2 courgettes (zucchini), sliced
2 celery sticks (stalks), sliced
1 small bunch spring onions (scallions), chopped

Store cupboard ingredients
dried bay leaves
dried basil
cardamom pods
cumin seeds
healing water (see p. 25)
green olive oil
seaweed flakes

Though the base, or root, chakra is associated with the colour red, this green diet has the effect of warming this chakra, giving you that comforted and loved feeling. Your base chakra is the home of your kundalini energy. By practising the *mool bandh*, or the *Root Lock* (see p. 30) you close the three lower chakras so that the energy cannot be lost through the base of the spine.

Make this stew to eat on cold, wintery evenings, and feel yourself bathed in the warmth as it spreads from your base.

- Place the mung beans in a bowl and cover with water. Soak overnight.
- Drain the beans, then boil for 1 hour or until cooked, but still a little crunchy.
- In a heavy saucepan, dry-roast the pepper and courgette until slightly charred. Add the celery and cook until al dente.
- Add 1 mudra pinch cumin seeds, 5 small gyan pinches dried basil and 4 or 5 cardamom pods. Stir for a few minutes, pulling the *mool bandh* as you stir. Add 2 bay leaves and enough healing water to form a soupy base.
- Add the cooked mung beans plus additional water if required to cover the ingredients. Boil for half an hour, adjusting the water as you go along to keep the ingredients covered. Once cooked, add the chopped spring onions, but just before serving.
- To serve, garnish with a few swirls of green olive oil and a generous sprinkling of seaweed flakes. Serve piping hot.

Sat Nam

Spicy spinach pancakes

You will need
1 small cucumber, grated
1 large bunch spinach
2 double handfuls rice flour
1 double handful rice milk
1 handful desiccated (shredded) coconut
3 mild green chillies, finely chopped
1 thumb-length nub fresh ginger root, grated

Store cupboard ingredients
salt
sugar
green olive oil
healing water (see p. 25)

Making pancakes is a very nurturing activity as the attention required infuses the food with your *prana* and good thoughts. So, whilst making this dish think of love, warmth, affection, friendship and also put in a wish for the future. When your family and friends eat the pancakes they will incorporate these intentions into their physical beings.

This dish includes rice milk, rice flour and desiccated coconut, therefore is not strictly a Green Diet dish. We have included it here because it goes beautifully with Panj Piare Okra (see p. 36).

- Grate the cucumber and finely chop the spinach.
- Add the rice flour, rice milk, desiccated coconut, chilli and grated ginger along with 1 small gyan pinch each of salt and sugar and 2 or 3 circular swirls of olive oil.
- Mix together well, then add the healing water. Start with 1 double handful, adding more as required to make a thick batter. Stand for 15–20 minutes.
- Mould the mixture in your hands, squeezing out any excess liquid.
- Heat a non-stick frying pan until hot, then place the uncooked pancakes in the pan. Using your fingers and repeated strokes, spread the mixture out until each is approximately 1 cm (½ in) thick.
- Cook until the underside is no longer runny. Flip over and cook for another 3 minutes.
- Serve warm as part of a meal or enjoy as a delicious snack during your day.

Sat Nam

Holy spinach and herb salad

You will need
3 double handfuls baby spinach
1 small bunch fresh parsley
1 small bunch fresh coriander (cilantro)
1 small bunch fresh basil
1 double handful sugar snap (sugar) peas
1 avocado, sliced into half moons
juice of 1 lemon

Store cupboard ingredients
green olive oil
tamari soy sauce
sea salt

(pictured on page 28)

This dish is a fresh and lively mix for everyday eating. We suggest you chant *Ang Sang Wahe Guru as* you prepare this salad, infusing it with the energy of this mantra. *Wahe Guru* means 'Great beyond description is his wisdom'. The chant *Ang Sang Wahe Guru* means 'The dynamic, living ecstasy of the universe is dancing within every cell of me' – it should be chanted with your heart lifted to receive.

- Steam the spinach just long enough to wilt the leaves.
- Tear the fresh herbs with your hands and mix through the spinach, then sprinkle on the sugar snap peas.
- Add the slices of avocado and 3 swirls of olive oil, tracing the outline of the infinity symbol as you do. Squeeze the lemon juice directly on to the salad, and add tamari or sea salt, to taste.
- Eat this dish with smiles as a whole meal or as a side dish.

Sat Nam

Green chilli and lentil soup

You will need
2 double handfuls green lentils (soaked or sprouted)
7 celery sticks (stalks), sliced
2 spring onions (scallions), chopped
7 broccoli florets
2 small green chillies, chopped
1 handful fresh coriander (cilantro), chopped

Store cupboard ingredients
yogic spice (see p. 27)
yogic stock cube (see p. 27)
tamari soy sauce
green olive oil

(pictured on page 28)

This soup is both energising and cleansing, which means strong *prana* (life force) and strong *apana* (eliminative force). By mixing both the *prana* and *apana*, we generate huge pressure, which raises the kundalini energy from the root chakra. We suggest you do the *Conquer Inner Anger and Burn It Out* meditation (see p. 154) before you start preparing the soup, and again, before serving.

- Soak the lentils for a few hours before making this dish or use sprouted lentils.
- Place the celery and spring onions in a heated saucepan and stir, tracing the outline of a triangle, until the juices seep from the vegetables. Add a few drops of water as you stir, as required. Add the broccoli and keep stirring.
- Once combined, add the drained lentils, chopped chillies and 1 mudra pinch of yogic spice. Stir a further 4 times. Now add enough water to triple the amount of lentils and vegetables in the saucepan. Add 1 stock cube, crushed between your fingers, and season with tamari, to taste.
- Cover and cook over a low heat until the lentils are tender – for unsprouted lentils this will take approximately 30–40 minutes.
- Serve each bowl of soup topped with a sprinkle of chopped coriander and an 'infinity' swirl of green olive oil.

Sat Nam

Ratatouille aad guray nameh

You will need
- 1 double handful mung beans (soaked or sprouted)
- 1 medium broccoli head, broken into florets
- 1 small green cabbage, sliced
- 7 celery sticks (stalks), sliced
- 4 garlic cloves, crushed
- 1 handful fresh basil leaves, torn
- 1 thumb-length nub fresh ginger root, grated
- 3 green tomatoes, diced
- 1 handful fresh thyme, finely chopped

Optional
- 2 courgettes (zucchini), sliced
- 1 green (bell) pepper, seeded and sliced

Store cupboard ingredients
- yogic or organic stock (bouillon) cube (see p. 27)
- seaweed flakes
- green olive oil
- fennel seeds

This is a traditional French dish, with a kundalini twist. *Aad Guray Nameh* is a *Mangala Charan* mantra that clears away doubt and opens you to guidance and protection, surrounding the human magnetic field with protective light. We often chant this mantra at the beginning of a gathering or when people are embarking on a journey (see p. 155).

- Soak the mung beans for a few hours before making this dish, or use sprouted mung beans.
- Drain the mung beans, if using unsprouted, and put them in a saucepan with 3 double handfuls of healing water – this is 1 part beans to 3 parts water. Bring to the boil and cook for 1½ hours, or until al dente. Drain and set aside.
- Steam the broccoli, green cabbage, celery, garlic and basil (keeping a few basil leaves for garnish) in a bamboo steamer until tender. The level of water in the saucepan should be half that of the quantity of the vegetables used.
- Whilst the vegetables are steaming, brush the courgette circles and pepper slices with olive oil and chargrill until blackened (optional).
- Remove the steamer with the vegetables and set aside.
- Add the drained mung beans to the water used to steam the vegetables. Cook until the mung beans are soft, but not mushy.
- Add the steamed vegetables, along with the ginger, green tomatoes, thyme and 1 stock cube. Mix everything together, stirring 31 times in a circular motion chanting the *Aad Guray Nameh* mantra at the same time.
- To serve, sprinkle 2 mudra pinches of seaweed flakes over the dish and 1 or 2 swirls of olive oil. Top with the grilled vegetables, if using. Garnish with the remaining strips of fresh basil leaves and 1 small gyan pinch of fennel seeds, crushed. Serve on warmed plates.

Sat Nam

Zucchini akal takht

You will need
4 sheets of lasagne verde
2 bunches spring onions (scallions), chopped
3 courgettes (zucchini), sliced
1 small mild green chilli
1 small handful green olives, sliced
1 handful fresh mint, chopped
juice of 2 limes
6 medium green tomatoes, sliced

Store cupboard ingredients
green olive oil
dried marjoram
dried cumin seeds
green peppercorns, crushed

Akal Takht, 'Eternal Throne', refers to the seat of temporal and spiritual authority in the holy city of Amritsar, Punjab, northern India. It was constructed by the sixth Guru, Hargobind, in 1609. At the place where the Akal Takht currently stands was a playground where the Guru played as a child – it was here also that he was installed as the sixth Guru on the death of his father, Guru Arjan Dev, in 1606. In this dish, the lasagne forms the throne on which the goodness of the vegetables and herbs sit.

- Heat the oven to 180°C/350°F/gas mark 4.
- Prepare the sheets of lasagne verde according to the instructions on the packet.
- Over a medium heat, sauté the spring onions until translucent in a few splashes of olive oil.
- Add the zucchini and 1 mudra pinch of dried marjoram. Cook until the zucchini slices are just tender.
- Add the chilli, olives, mint, lime juice and 1 mudra pinch of cumin seeds. Season with crushed green peppercorns, to taste. Continue cooking until everything is heated through.
- Layer the mixture in a casserole dish with the sliced tomatoes and the lasagne verde, starting with a layer of lasagne verde and finishing with a layer of vegetable mixture.
- Place in the oven and bake for approximately 22 minutes.
- While the dish is in the oven, do the *Healing the Stomach Kriya* (p. 145) to let the sun shine within you, circulating the energy inside you, in readiness to receive this wonderful, wholesome meal.

Sat Nam

Panj piare okra

You will need
garlic shoots from 1 garlic bulb, finely chopped
1 bunch fresh basil leaves, roughly chopped
1–2 green chillies, finely diced, to taste
4 generous handfuls okra
1 bunch fresh mint, roughly chopped
1 bunch fresh dill, finely chopped

Store cupboard ingredients
green olive oil

Panj Piare, 'Five Beloved Ones', originally referred to the five men who volunteered to give their lives when the Khalsa was founded in 1699 (see p. 38). Nowadays five people, symbolising the Panj Piare, officiate at the Khalsa, initiate ceremonies and other special occasions. In this recipe it refers to the garlic shoots, basil, dill, mint and green chillies that give this dish its strong, potent taste.

- In a large frying pan, sauté the garlic shoots, basil and finely diced chilli in a few drops of water until you achieve a paste-like consistency. Add more water as required to form the paste.
- Drop in the okra and cook over a low heat until the paste reduces and sticks to the okra.
- Sprinkle over the fresh mint and dill. Swirl over 2 rounds of olive oil and toss through.
- When on the Green Diet, this dish is delicious with the Ek Ong Kar Salad (p. 41). If not on this diet, we suggest you try it with the Vegetable Salad with Kundalini Dressing (p. 133) or the Spicy Spinach Pancakes (see p. 33).

Sat Nam

TOP Zucchini akal takht
ABOVE Panj piare okra

Simran kale

You will need
12 generous handfuls kale
6 medium green tomatoes, diced
2 medium green onions, diced
½ green (bell) pepper, finely diced
1 small handful fresh coriander (cilantro) leaves
1 handful pistachio nuts, chopped

From the store cupboard
cumin seeds
seaweed flakes
crushed peppercorns

Kale is one of those 'difficult' to eat greens as it has a very strong taste. However, it is a rich source of dietary fibre, proteins, thiamin, riboflavin, folate, iron, magnesium and phosphorus, and contains a multitude of vitamins and minerals. If you really would prefer to not eat kale, despite its amazing nutritional value, this recipe also works well with collard, chard, beet greens, mustard greens or a combination of your choice.

Nam Simran is the devotional practice of meditating on the Divine name – being conscious of and attentive to God. So, when you are eating this dish, eat slowly and be conscious of the goodness you are putting into your body.

- Wash the greens. Remove any large stems and discoloured leaves. Slice the leaves lengthwise into finger-wide strips.
- Combine in a saucepan the tomatoes, onions and pepper with 1 mudra pinch each of cumin seeds and seaweed flakes. Cover and cook over a medium heat for 5 minutes.
- Add the kale and with the saucepan still covered, gently simmer, stirring frequently, for 10 to 15 minutes or until the leaves are tender. Whilst the vegetables are simmering meditate on your heart chakra.
- Add the crushed peppercorns to taste and serve garnished with roughly chopped coriander leaves and pistachio nuts.
- This dish is a lovely topping for the Spicy Spinach Pancakes (see p.33) and the Uddin Vade Patties (see p. 43).

Sat Nam

Baisakhi spinach curry

You will need
6 medium green tomatoes
2 green chillies
green shoots from 1 garlic bulb
8 double handfuls fresh spinach, chopped

From the store cupboard
green olive oil
mustard seeds
cumin seeds
seaweed flakes

Baisakhi, celebrated each year on 13 April, is the birthdate of the Khalsa, the day that Guru Gobind Singh founded the Khalsa. Guru Gobind Singh was the last of the 10 Sikh Gurus. He was also a warrior who wanted his followers to excel in the martial arts so they could defend their families and people. On 30 March 1699 he organised a large gathering in the middle of a battlefield in the Punjabi town of Anandpur. At this gathering he asked for volunteers prepared to sacrifice their lives for the future of his people – five men came forward.

The guru took them away to his tent and dressed them in glorious white. He baptised each of the men and, in turn, had them baptise him. 'Now you are my guru', he told them, and with that all Sikhs became equal and the Khalsa was formed. He took the surname Singh, which means 'lion', and gave this name to all Sikh men. The women were given the surname Kaur or 'princess'.

While pounding this dish to make a pulp, we recommend you put the energies of Guru Gobind Singh into your actions by chanting the *Chattr Chakkr Varti* (see p. 155).

- Pound the tomatoes, chillies and garlic shoots into a paste.
- Heat a couple of swirls of olive oil in a large frying pan over a medium heat until it is hot and starts to smoke.
- Add 3 small gyan pinches of mustard seeds and cook until they pop. Add the pounded tomato paste. Stir in a circular motion for 2 minutes.
- Add the spinach, 1 small gyan pinch of cumin seeds and 2 mudra pinches of seaweed flakes. Stir well and reduce the heat to medium-low. Cover and cook for 5–8 minutes.
- Serve and celebrate the life of Guru Gobind Singh.

Sat Nam

Baisakhi spinach curry

Bountiful, blissful and beautiful salad

You will need
1 green (bell) pepper
1 small cucumber
3 green tomatoes
1 bunch spring onions (scallions)
3 green chillies
1 bunch fresh mint
1 bunch fresh coriander (cilantro)
1 handful fresh basil leaves
other green herbs of your choice
juice and rind (zest) of 1 lime

From the store cupboard
green olive oil

This salad is about feeling good. Bountiful, blissful and beautiful is the mantra of bliss and the affirmation of the Divine Self and this salad embodies this spirit. It is created from the bountiful green vegetables and herbs available to us that are blissful to our bodies, and is a beautiful dish – and its secret is the very liberal use of herbs for flavouring. As a general rule of thumb, have an equal ratio of herbs to vegetables.

Whilst preparing this salad sing, 'I am bountiful, blissful and beautiful; bountiful, blissful and beautiful I am.' Sing loudly, experimenting with your own tunes.

- Dice the pepper, cucumber and tomatoes into small cubes. Slice the spring onions.
- Roughly chop the chillies and herbs, including the stalks. Add them to the diced vegetables.
- To finish, squeeze the lime juice over the salad. Drizzle lightly with olive oil and scatter over the coarsely grated lime rind.

Sat Nam

Hum dum har har tomatoes

You will need
4–6 green tomatoes

From the store cupboard
green olive oil
seaweed flakes

Hum Dum Har Har (We the universe, God, God) is a mantra that opens the heart chakra – and the green of the green tomatoes in this dish are the colour of this chakra. This is a very simple and elegant dish, with the tomatoes forming a *kara* – a thin steel circle worn on the wrist, representing truth and freedom.

- Heat on a high setting a heavy pan or griddle and lightly brush it with olive oil.
- Slice the tomatoes into 4–6 thick circles, depending on their size. Add to the pan.
- Cook until the undersides of the tomatoes are a golden colour. Turn over and cook the other side.
- Add seaweed flakes to taste and serve immediately.

Sat Nam

Ek ong kar salad

You will need
4 generous handfuls watercress
4 generous handfuls mixed salad leaves
1 large bunch green grapes, seedless
2 avocados, diced
2 kiwi fruits, diced
2 green apples, diced
squeeze of lemon juice

From the store cupboard
green olive oil

The various Kundalini Yoga diets have been around for centuries – food was mentioned in the ancient yogi literatures. A yogi is concerned with the subtle effects that food has on his mind and astral body, and therefore advocates pure, simple and fresh foods. This is the law the Ek Ong Kar Salad embraces.

The mantra *Ek Ong Kar Satgur Parsaad* (see p. 155) is about elevating the self beyond duality, and establishes the flow of the spirit. Chant it with great reverence while making this dish.

- Line a serving platter or individual salad plates with the watercress and salad leaves.
- Cut the grapes in half and dice the other fruit and vegetables. Arrange these over the salad greens.
- Dress with a swirl of olive oil and a squeeze of lime juice.

Sat Nam

Pranic green juice

You will need
2 small green apples
1 small cucumber
12 celery sticks (stalks)
4–5 large handfuls spinach
4 kale leaves
1 handful fresh parsley

From the store cupboard
seaweed flakes

No treatise on the Green Diet is complete without at least one mention of wheatgrass, the nectar of rejuvenation, the plasma of youth and the blood of all life. Wheatgrass juice is one of the best sources of living chlorophyll available, and as chlorophyll is the primary product of light, it contains more light energy than any other element. High in oxygen, enzymes, vitamins and nucleic acids, 25 millilitres (1 ounce) of wheatgrass juice contains more nutrients than 1 kilogram (2 pounds) of fresh vegetables. The Pranic Green Juice is an energy-loaded alternative; however, for an even greater boost, you can always also add wheatgrass and make a 'super drink'.

- Core the apples and put into a food processor. Add the vegetables and 1 mudra pinch of seaweed flakes. Process until you achieve a smooth drinking consistency.
- To gain maximum energy from this juice, drink it with your friends and family immediately.

Sat Nam

Avocado and grape namaskar

You will need
2 ripe avocados
1 large bunch green grapes, seedless
4 celery sticks (stalks) (optional)
iceberg lettuce leaves (optional)

From the store cupboard
seaweed flakes

The practice of *Surya Namaskar*, or Sun Salutation, is ubiquitous in yoga. It is a sequence of 12 *asanas* that draw peace, harmony and strength into the body in preparation for a yoga practice session. Both physically and spiritually uplifting, *Surya Namaskar* is a wholly satisfying practice. It nurtures the higher emotions of love, peace and compassion, and brings about a sense of harmony and wellbeing.

- Place the flesh of the avocados and the grapes into a food processor and blend until smooth.
- Spoon into 4 small ramekins. Alternatively, spoon into 1 large dish that has been lined with clear film (plastic wrap). Chill for several hours, turn out, remove the clear film and slice.
- If serving with celery, cut the celery sticks into 12 'boats', each representing an *asana* of the *Surya Namaskar*. Fill each stick with the pâté.
- If serving with lettuce, make 12 parcels by wrapping spoonfuls of pâté in the lettuce leaves.

Sat Nam

Uddin vade patties

You will need
1 double handful green dhal (green lentils)
1 handful fresh coriander leaves (cilantro), chopped
2–3 small green chillies, finely diced

From the store cupboard
green peppercorns
sea salt
green olive oil
tamari

For the Baby Green and Sesame Salad (optional)
4 double handfuls green salad leaves
1 handful fresh coriander (cilantro)
juice of 1 lime
sesame seeds, toasted

Uddin Vade Patties are delicious, portable morsels, suitable for picnics and other gatherings with family and friends. They are also a great meal to serve with a seletion of green salads at an impromptu get together.

- Soak the dhal for 6 hours. Drain and then grind it with 1 mudra pinch of green peppercorns to form a smooth dough.
- Add the chopped coriander leaves and chillies. Season with sea salt, to taste.
- Mould a generous spoonful of the dough in your palm to make the patties. Repeat until you have used up all the mixture.
- Heat a splattering of olive oil in a frying pan over a medium-high setting. You will need to add more oil, as required, when cooking the patties.
- Carefully drop the patties into the heated oil and fry on both sides until they are golden brown and very fragrant.
- Serve as a filling snack with pickled green chillies or with a Baby Green and Sesame Salad (see below) as a complete meal – omit the sesame seeds if you are on the Green Diet.
- **Baby Green and Sesame Salad:** roughly chop the coriander and mix with the green salad leaves. Sprinkle with lime juice, olive oil, toasted sesame seeds and tamari, to taste.

Sat Nam

TOP Rainbow vegetable and herb salad (see p. 46)
ABOVE Purple onion soup (see p. 59)
RIGHT Aura-white mushroom and cauliflower pie (see p. 59)

4 Food for the chakras

Food to open the petals of your energy centres

Chakras are spinning energy centres. Within the human body there are seven major chakras located along the central energy channel, the *sushumna*, which rises up through the spine. Each chakra corresponds to a different area of the body, certain behavioural characteristics and spiritual growth in specific ways. In Kundalini Yoga, techniques are used to concentrate 'life force' in the *sushumna* and raise the kundalini energy through the seven chakras, from the root chakra, located at the very base of the spine, through to the crown chakra, situated at the front and top of the head.

When the kundalini energy is raised along the *sushumna* it pierces, activates and opens the chakras in its path – their levels of activity range from under-active to over-active. Ideally, all your chakras are open and balanced, at which time your instincts work together with your feelings and thoughts, and the *Shakti*, or female energy sleeping in your base chakra, is awakened and united with her beloved *Siva*, the male energy resident in your crown chakra.

Colour is visible sound – a form of energy that vibrates. As these sound vibrations become higher and lighter the different colours of the colour spectrum are formed. As you move up along the *sushumna*, the vibrational frequency of each chakra increases, and each chakra takes on a different colour of the colour spectrum.

Like the chakras, food is richly coloured with different levels of energy vibrations. This chapter is about the relationship between food and the chakras; it is about eating to help you balance your chakras for a happier, healthier and holier life.

Rainbow vegetable and herb salad

You will need
2 tomatoes, diced
1 red pepper, de-seeded and diced
1 yellow pepper, diced
2 carrots, diced
2 small cucumbers, diced
4 small radishes, diced
1 purple onion, diced
2 handfuls baby salad greens
1 handful cauliflower florets
1 handful fresh parsley, chopped
1 handful fresh basil, chopped
fresh lemon juice (or apple cider vinegar)
2 garlic cloves, finely chopped

From the store cupboard
olive oil
honey

(pictured on page 44)

For this dish we combine a broad selection of vegetables, their different colours reflecting the different colours of the seven primary chakras. Red is for the first chakra, orange is for the second chakra, yellow is for the third chakra, green is for the fourth chakra, and purple and white represent the fifth, the sixth and the seventh chakras. When eating this salad, not only will you enjoy its abundance, you will also enhance your chakras.

The mantra we suggest for this dish is *Har Har*: *Har* is one of the aspects of God – the creative Infinity. Chant it as you prepare the vegetables, using your navel centre to give power to every syllable and to help pronounce them clearly.

- Place the diced tomatoes, red and yellow peppers, carrots, cucumbers, radishes and onion, in a salad bowl. Add the baby salad greens and cauliflower florets.
- Sprinkle on the chopped parsley and basil, then mix through the vegetables with your hands, tracing the outline of the infinity symbol as you do. Set side.
- Pour the dressing (see below) over the salad and gently toss it through, using your hands.
- **To make the dressing:** take a small glass jar with a screw-top lid. Fill it with equal portions of olive oil and fresh lemon juice or apple cider vinegar – as an alternative you can also use a combination of both lemon juice and vinegar. Add the finely chopped garlic and 1 spoonful of honey. Seal the jar tightly and shake vigorously until the ingredients are well combined.

Sat Nam

Sun polenta with rainbow vegetables

You will need
1 beetroot (beet)
2 carrots
1 sweet potato (yam)
1 yellow pepper
1 fennel bulb
1 small broccoli head
1 red onion
7 garlic cloves
1 thumb-length nub fresh ginger root
1 handful baby spinach leaves
1 handful fresh basil leaves, roughly chopped
1 handful rocket (argula) leaves
juice of 1 lemon

Yogis have their equivalent to fast food, too, but to them fast food means food that is cooked quickly, preserving the tastes and nutrients. This is an example of a healthy fast food made with polenta.

For centuries polenta was the staple winter-time food of the poor in many countries across the globe. Its solidity and its use as a staple throughout the times, reinforces its quality as a foundation for survival, habit and self-acceptance – these are all qualities of the base, or root, chakra.

- Peel and dice the beetroot, carrots and sweet potato, quarter and de-seed the yellow pepper, slice the fennel bulb, break the broccoli head into florets, dice the onion and garlic and finely grate the fresh ginger.
- Place all the prepared vegetables in a bamboo steamer over a saucepan of simmering healing water. The quantity of water in the saucepan should be 2 double handfuls – by volume, this is equal to half the amount of polenta used in this recipe.

From the store cupboard
healing water (see p. 25)
almonds
paprika
celery powder
4 single handfuls fine organic polenta
tamari soy sauce
balsamic vinegar
olive oil

Note: 2 double handfuls liquid equals 250 ml, 8 fl oz and 1 cup

- Steam the vegetables until tender. Remove the steamer from the saucepan and transfer the vegetables to a glass bowl.
- Whilst the vegetables are steaming soak 9 almonds in boiling water for 1 minute. Drain, peel, roughly chop and dry-roast in a frying pan over a high heat until lightly browned. Set aside.
- Using the same saucepan and water as used to steam the vegetables, add enough paprika to turn the water sunset-red in colour. Add 1 mudra pinch of celery powder.
- With the heat set to low, slowly pour in the polenta. Then, with a wooden spoon, stir constantly in a clockwise direction for 11 minutes or until the polenta is set and creamy.
- Next, add the roughly chopped basil leaves to the steamed vegetables along with the baby spinach and rocket. Gently toss.
- Squeeze the lemon juice on the vegetables and drizzle over one and a half rounds of olive oil. Sprinkle the vegetables with both the tamari and the balsamic vinegar, to taste. Toss until well coated.
- Spread the cooked polenta over the middle of a serving plate. Spoon on the vegetables, then sprinkle on the roasted almonds.

Sat Nam

Sun polenta with rainbow vegetables

Buckwheat harmony

You will need
1 garlic clove, finely chopped
1 thumb-length nub fresh ginger root, finely grated
1 onion, diced
4 courgettes (zucchini), sliced
4 celery sticks (stalks), sliced
1 double handful buckwheat
1 handful fresh mint leaves, chopped
1 handful basil leaves, chopped
1 handful baby spinach leaves

From the store cupboard
olive oil
ground cumin
paprika
yogic or organic stock (bouillon) cubes (see p. 27)
healing water (see p. 25)
tamari soy sauce

Buckwheat, used as a staple food for thousands of years, is related to the rhubarb plant as opposed to the wheat grain. This means it is a good, mineral-rich substitute for anyone who suffers from a wheat allergy or gluten intolerance.

Diets that contain buckwheat have been linked with reducing the risk of developing high cholesterol and high blood pressure. Therefore, on a physical level, this dish helps the heart to stay healthy. On an energetic level, the green of the vegetables and herbs harmonise the green energy of the heart chakra.

- Sauté the garlic, ginger and onion with 3 swirls of olive oil in a large saucepan over a low heat.
- Add the sliced courgettes and celery sticks. Tracing the outline of the infinity symbol, mix the ingredients for 11 minutes.
- Add 1 mudra pinch each of the ground cumin and paprika.
- Add the buckwheat, 2 stock cubes and 4 double handfuls of healing water. Bring to the boil. Add the mint, basil and baby spinach leaves, keeping 1 pinch of mint and 1 pinch of basil aside for garnish.
- Simmer over a low heat until all the liquid is absorbed. This will take about 30 minutes. Season with tamari.
- Transfer the mixture to a serving dish and garnish it with the remaining mint and basil.

Sat Nam

Tomato, basil and gobinde tofu salad

You will need
1 large block tofu (450 g/1 lb)
juice of 1 lemon
8 ripe tomatoes
16 basil leaves

From the store cupboard
olive oil
tamari soy sauce
dried mint
dried oregano

Makes 16 portions

This is a classic yogic dish that is strongly influenced by Mediterranean cuisine. The tomato is for the base chakra, the basil is for the heart chakra and the tofu is for the aura – they come together to make a beautiful and bountiful dish.

- Cut the tofu into slices about ¾-cm (¼-in) thick. Place in a glass bowl and marinate with the lemon juice, 4 swirls of olive oil, 8 drops of tamari, and 1 mudra pinch each of dried mint and dried oregano for 22 minutes.
- Remove the tofu slices from the marinade and place under a moderately hot grill. Grill until they are crisp on both sides. Turn the slices only once.
- Slice the tomato – depending on their size, you should get approximately 32 slices in total.
- Sandwich 1 slice of tofu and 1 basil leaf between 2 slices of tomato.
- Drizzle over the marinade before serving.

Sat Nam

TOP Buckwheat harmony
ABOVE Tomato, basil and gobinde tofu salad

Carrot and sweet potato pilaf

You will need
1 onion, peeled and chopped
4 garlic cloves, chopped
2 carrots, cut into julienne
1 sweet potato (yam), peeled and thinly sliced
3 handfuls bulgur (cracked wheat)
1 handful fresh mint, chopped

From the store cupboard
olive oil
yogic or organic stock (bouillon) cubes (see p. 27)
healing water (see p. 25)
tamari soy sauce

To honour the femininity and grace of the second, or sacral, chakra, sing the *Adi Shakti* mantra (see p. 155) as you prepare this dish. This mantra celebrates the *Shakti*, the goddess in all, and is a powerful accompaniment to this dish.

- Sauté the onion and garlic with 3 swirls of olive oil and a few drops of water in a large frying pan over a medium heat. Add the carrots and sweet potato. Mix well.
- Add the bulgur, 2 stock cubes and 2 double handfuls healing water. Stir until the stock cubes dissolve. Mix through the chopped fresh mint – keep a few pinches aside for garnish.
- Bring the mixture to the boil. Lower the heat and simmer for 11 minutes, or until all the liquid is absorbed.
- Season with 1 swirl of tamari and garnish with the remaining mint leaves.

Sat Nam

Yellow pepper and soya bean yogic stew

You will need
4 handfuls soya beans
3 spring onions (scallions), finely chopped
9 garlic cloves, crushed
1 thumb-length nub fresh ginger root, finely grated
1 yellow pepper, chopped
1 handful yellow beans, roughly chopped

From the store cupboard
turmeric
ground cumin
healing water (see p. 25)
yogic or organic stock (bouillon) cubes (see p. 27)
olive oil
sea salt

The third, or navel, chakra is about action and balance. With its concentration of yellow-coloured ingredients – the colour of the third chakra – this is a wonderful dish to serve either when the energy of this chakra needs to be enhanced or when you want to relax and heal your emotions.

- Soak the soya beans in plenty of water overnight – they should remain covered at all times. Drain, rinse and place in a large saucepan with fresh water. Bring to the boil, then turn the heat down and cook until the soya beans are tender. This will take 2–3 hours.
- In a saucepan, dry-fry the spring onion, garlic and ginger with 1 mudra pinch each of turmeric and cumin over a medium heat until aromatic.
- Add the yellow pepper and yellow beans and stir 8 times, tracing the outline of a triangle. Add the cooked and drained soya beans.
- Add enough healing water to cover the ingredients. Crumble over 1 stock cube and mix through. Cover the saucepan and simmer for 22 minutes.
- Transfer the ingredients to 4 serving dishes. Season each with 1 swirl of olive oil and a sprinkling of sea salt.

Sat Nam

Corn bread with seeds and feta

You will need
4 single handfuls cornmeal
4 single handfuls wholemeal flour
2 double handfuls milk
1 small green pepper, finely chopped
1 handful feta cheese

From the store cupboard
sea salt
baking powder
olive oil
sesame and sunflower seeds
turmeric
honey

Note: 2 double handfuls liquid equals 250 ml, 8 fl oz and 1 cup

This dish is for the third, or navel, chakra, which is the centre of personal power and commitment. It also embodies the will of the spiritual warrior. We serve this bread either for breakfast or for lunch with a salad to help create balance and to enhance and energise both the third chakra and the whole body. For added energy, chant *Wha-Hay Guroo* as you make the batter.

- Pre-heat the oven to 180°C/350°F/gas mark 4.
- Mix the cornmeal and wholemeal flour together in a bowl. Add 1 mudra pinch of sea salt and 2 mudra pinches of baking powder. Continue to mix until all the ingredients are well combined.
- Slowly add 1 double handful of olive oil and approximately 2 double handfuls of milk. Add the milk in stages, beating well between each addition. The batter should be thick, so adjust the quantity of milk used, as required. Beat together until you get a smooth batter.
- Fold through the green pepper, 1 single handful of a mixture of sesame and sunflower seeds, the feta cubes, 1 mudra pinch of turmeric and 1 generous swirl of honey.
- Line a 24-cm (9-in) round baking tin with baking paper. Pour in the batter.
- Place the tin in the pre-heated oven and bake for 31 minutes or until the corn bread is firm to touch and golden on top. Alternately, test if cooked by inserting a skewer into the middle of the corn bread. It should come out clean.
- Serve hot, cold with salad or on its own.

Sat Nam

Kundalini chakra and blood-cleansing salad

You will need
1 thumb-length nub fresh ginger root, grated
1 garlic clove, crushed
1 red onion, diced
1 red apple, diced
1 red pepper, de-seeded and diced
1 small red chilli, finely chopped
1 red tomato, diced
juice of 1 small orange

From the store cupboard
olive oil
apple cider vinegar
sea salt

A traditional Western saying is that an apple a day keeps the doctor away. In the Kundalini Yoga tradition it is the humble onion, combined with ginger and garlic, that keeps us healthy – the apple is also considered to be very healing. When feeling unwell, the most effective way for many people to begin the healing process is with a 'cleanse' – a holistic approach that allows the body to heal itself, naturally.

- Grate the ginger, finely chop the garlic and dice the onion, apple, de-seeded red pepper, chilli and tomato.
- Pour the orange juice over the vegetables. Add 1 generous swirl of olive oil, 1 swirl of vinegar, and 1 small gyan pinch of sea salt. Toss, then marinate for at least 11 minutes.
- When mixing the ingredients chant a long *Ong* for the infinite connection with the base chakra – this will be balanced by the red vegetables and red apple.

Sat Nam

TOP Corn bread with seeds and feta
ABOVE Kundalini chakra and blood-cleansing salad

Heart chakra broccoli and potato cream soup

You will need
1 leek, sliced
1 onion, sliced
2 broccoli heads, broken into florets
4 potatoes, peeled and diced
fresh parsley (for garnish)
fresh mint (for garnish)

From the store cupboard
olive oil
yogic spice or garam masala (see p. 27)
turmeric
paprika
ground cumin
red chilli flakes
healing water (see p. 25)
yogic or organic stock (bouillon) cubes (see p. 27)
sea salt

As this soup is for the fourth, or heart, chakra, we recommend you chant the mantra *Humee Hum Brahm Hum* during its preparation. *Hum* is the sound associated with the heart chakra, and by chanting this mantra you will open this chakra and activate its connection with the fifth, or throat, chakra.

- Sauté the leek and onion with 1 swirl of olive oil in a large saucepan over a low heat.
- Add the broccoli florets and diced potatoes. Stir, tracing the outline of a triangle, for 11 minutes.
- Add 1 mudra pinch each yogic spice (or garam masala), turmeric, paprika, ground cumin and red chilli flakes. Mix well.
- Cover the vegetables with healing water. Crumble over 1 stock cube and stir until it is dissolved. Bring to the boil, then simmer for 15 minutes, or until the vegetables are tender.
- Transfer the soup mixture to a food processor. Blend until smooth.
- Pour the puréed vegetables back into the saucepan. Add 3 swirls of olive oil, season with sea salt and reheat until hot.
- To serve, garnish with roughly chopped fresh parsley or a sprig of mint.

Sat Nam

Spinach celery pie with fresh herbs

You will need
7 celery sticks (stalks), finely sliced
1 onion, finely sliced
7 handfuls baby spinach
2 handfuls fresh herbs (mint, basil, parsley and coriander [cilantro])
2 handfuls wholemeal flour
Green Sauce (see p. 104)

From the store cupboard
tamari soy sauce
olive oil
yogic spice or garam masala (see p. 27)

The heart chakra is the unifying centre for the lower and upper chakras. It is about sacred transformation and awakening to spiritual awareness. It is also about heaven and earth coming together in perfect balance, the merging of two qualities. By combining two elements and blurring the boundaries, we are at One. In this dish, the heavenliness and the earthiness of the wholemeal flour is merged harmoniously with the more ethereal greens to give you a lovely, satisfying and balanced dish.

- Pre-heat the oven to 180°C/350°F/gas mark 4.
- Put the sliced celery sticks and onion, the baby spinach and the mixed herbs in a bamboo steamer over a saucepan of simmering water. Steam until the vegetables are soft.
- Transfer the vegetables and herbs to a bowl and mash.
- Add the wholemeal flour, 18 drops of tamari, 4 swirls of olive oil and 1 mudra pinch of yogic spice or garam masala. Mix well.
- Place a thin layer of the mix in a 30x8x3-cm (12x8x3-in) baking tray lined with baking paper. Alternatively you can make individual patties using small 10-cm (4-in) round pastry cases.
- Place the tray in the oven and bake for 31 minutes or until golden brown on top.
- Serve warm with a fresh green salad and Green Sauce.

Sat Nam

Salad greens and cabbage heart chakra salad

You will need
1 cabbage, finely sliced
4 handfuls baby salad greens
1 small green chilli, finely chopped
mint leaves (for garnish)

From the store cupboard
olive oil
tamari soy sauce
rice vinegar

The heart chakra manifests itself in the colour green and green energy – the energy of the sun. Cabbage is widely used for losing weight, but its high beta-carotene and potassium content is often overlooked. It also contains phyto-chemicals, such as glucosinolates, that are proven to help reduce the possibility of developing cancer.

As you slice the cabbage, chant *Ong So Hung*. *Ong* means creative consciousness and *So Hung* means 'I am Thou' – chanting the word *Hung* stimulates and opens the heart chakra.

- Finely slice the cabbage and place it in a bowl together with the washed baby salad greens. Toss three times with your hands to help manifest the physical, emotional/mental and spiritual states.
- Add 3 swirls of olive oil and 18 drops each of tamari and rice vinegar.
- Finely chop the small green chilli and mix it through the salad. Cover, set aside and let the ingredients marinate for at least 3 hours – for a truly wonderful and energising dish marinate for 11 hours, or overnight, in a cool place away from direct sunlight.
- To serve, mix again and sprinkle with fresh mint leaves.

Sat Nam

Crown chakra adzuki bean casserole

You will need
2 handfuls adzuki beans
2 white onions, diced
7 garlic cloves, crushed
1 red chilli, chopped
1 green chilli, chopped
4 carrots, sliced
2 celery sticks (stalks), finely diced
4 tomatoes, peeled and diced
fresh parsley (for garnish)

From the store cupboard
olive oil
bay leaves
turmeric
paprika
ground cumin
yogic or organic stock (bouillon) cubes (see p. 27)
healing water (see p. 25)

The crown chakra is the seventh chakra – it is the easiest to visualise as it is the aura located at the front and top of the head. We use the adzuki beans for this dish because they contain purple phyto-chemicals, which help clear the mind and balance the pituitary glands. Adzuki beans give the physical body energy. They are also an excellent source of soluble fibre, which has been shown to lower serum cholesterol and to help stabilise blood sugar levels.

- Soak the adzuki beans in plenty of water for 2 hours.
- Drain the beans and put in a saucepan. Fill the saucepan with water – 1 part beans to 3 parts water. Bring to the boil and cook for 1 hour. Drain and rinse.
- Sauté the white onions and garlic with 3 swirls of olive oil in a saucepan over a medium heat. Add the chopped chillies, carrots and celery stalks and 2 bay leaves. Continue to sauté until the vegetables are tender.
- Add the diced tomatoes and 1 mudra pinch each of turmeric, paprika and ground cumin.
- Add the cooked adzuki beans, then pour in enough healing water to completely cover all the ingredients. Crumble over 1 stock cube and mix by tracing the outline of the infinity symbol.
- Bring to the boil, reduce the heat, cover and simmer for 31 minutes.
- To serve, garnish with chopped fresh parsley.

Sat Nam

Kundalini root chakra beetroot steam

You will need
4 beetroots (beet), peeled and sliced
1 purple onion, sliced
8 garlic cloves, thinly sliced
juice of 1 lemon
1 orange, peeled and cut into segments
1 handful fresh coriander (cilantro) leaves, roughly chopped (optional)

From the store cupboard
olive oil
sea salt
cayenne pepper

The root, or first, chakra is connected with grounding and elimination; its associated colour is dark red. The beetroot (beet) is representative of this chakra both in colour and its nutritional properties. It provides a good source of anthocyanins, a natural antioxidant that contributes to its deep red colour, and it is often used for elimination and detoxification.

- Place the beetroot, onion and garlic in a bamboo steamer over a saucepan of simmering water. Steam until tender.
- Remove from the steamer and arrange on a serving plate. Squeeze over the lemon juice.
- Drizzle on 3 swirls of olive oil and a sprinkling of sea salt, to taste.
- Garnish with the orange segments and the chopped fresh coriander (optional).
- Sprinkle with cayenne pepper and serve.

Sat Nam

Crown chakra stuffed purple cabbage

You will need
1 large purple cabbage
2 double handfuls quinoa
1 handful fresh basil
1 handful fresh parsley
1 purple onion, diced
1 finger-length nub fresh ginger root, finely grated
4 garlic cloves, finely diced
juice of 1 lemon

From the store cupboard
healing water (see p. 25)
yogic or organic stock (bouillon) cubes (see p. 27)
chopped mixed nuts
tamari soy sauce

This is a stunning dish that is easy to prepare and makes a great banquet centrepiece. The cabbage is a simple vegetable that encapsulates the crown, or seventh, chakra, which is about surrender – the humility that fills you as you bow before the Infinite.

- Pull off the individual leaves of the purple cabbage, taking care not to tear them. Place the leaves one on top of the other in a large saucepan. Pour on just-boiled healing water until they are completely covered, then soak until they soften.
- Place the quinoa, basil, parsley, diced purple onion, grated ginger and crushed garlic in a large saucepan with 4 cups of healing water and 2 crumbled stock cubes.
- Bring to the boil. Simmer until all the liquid is absorbed and the quinoa opens up. This will take 10–15 minutes.
- Remove the saucepan from the stove top. Stir in the chopped mixed nuts.
- Take a cabbage leaf in the palm of your hand and spoon in some of the quinoa filling. Roll up and place in a bamboo steamer. Repeat this process until you have used all the cabbage leaves and filling.
- Place the bamboo steamer over a saucepan of simmering water. Steam for 11 minutes.
- Place on a serving platter and drizzle over lemon juice and tamari, to taste. Serve with a fresh green salad.

Sat Nam

Purple onion soup

You will need
7 purple onions, diced
1 handful orange lentils (split red lentils)
1 handful fresh coriander (cilantro), chopped
juice of 1 lemon

From the store cupboard
olive oil
red chilli flakes
ground cumin
turmeric
healing water (see p. 25)
tamari soy sauce

(pictured on page 44)

This is a variation of French onion soup. Instead of cheese, normally melted on bread that is then placed in the bowl of soup, we use orange lentils. These bring both colour and balancing energy to the crown, or seventh, chakra.

- Sauté the onion with a swirl of olive oil in a large saucepan until soft.
- Add the lentils and 1 mudra pinch each of chilli flakes, cumin and turmeric. Mix by tracing the outline of the infinity symbol.
- Add enough healing water to double the level of the lentils and onion in the saucepan. Sprinkle over 11 drops of tamari, the fresh coriander and the lemon juice. Simmer until the lentils are cooked. This will take 21–31 minutes.
- Serve with 1 small swirl of olive oil and a sprinkling of chilli flakes in each bowl.

Sat Nam

Aura-white mushroom and cauliflower pie

You will need
1 handful flax seeds (linseeds)
18 mushrooms
1 cauliflower head, broken into florets
1 leek, diced
2 white onions, diced
8 garlic cloves, crushed
1 thumb length nub fresh ginger root, finely grated

For the sauce
2 handfuls (125 ml/4 fl oz) milk or rice milk
1 small gyan mudra pinch arrowroot powder
1 garlic clove, crushed

From the store cupboard
healing water (see p. 25)
olive oil
bay leaf
white peppercorns
wholemeal flour
sea salt
tamari soy sauce

(pictured on page 44)

The aura, or the eighth chakra, is the sum of all the seven main chakras. It is associated with the colour white and the basic principles of purity, new beginnings and deep cleansing. Serve this dish with white basmati rice and freshly grated radish, dressed with lemon juice and olive oil, which creates a unique flavour.

- Pre-heat the oven to 200°C/400°F/gas mark 6.
- Soak the flax seeds in an equal quantity of healing water to flax seeds for 11 minutes. When ready, place into a food processor and blend until you get a paste-like texture.
- Steam the mushrooms and cauliflower in a bamboo steamer over simmering water until tender.
- Heat a generous swirl of olive oil in a frying pan over a medium heat.
- Add the leek, white onion, garlic, ginger, 1 bay leaf and 3 white peppercorns. Sauté, tracing the outline of a triangle as you do so.
- Add 2 further swirls of olive oil and 2 single handfuls of wholemeal flour. Fold all the ingredients together.
- Add the flax seed purée and the steamed mushrooms and cauliflower. Combine well.
- Season with tamari or sea salt. Spoon into a 24-cm (9-in) pie dish and place into the oven. Cook for 31 minutes. The top should turn a beautiful, golden colour.
- Top with the white sauce (see below) and serve with your favourite salad or basmati rice and grated radish dressed with fresh lemon juice and olive oil.
- **For the sauce:** Place all the sauce ingredients in a small saucepan over a medium heat. Whisk until smooth and heated through. Season with sea salt, to taste.

Sat Nam

Steamed kohlrabi, parsnip and quinoa

You will need
4 kohlrabis (cabbage turnips), peeled and diced
4 parsnips, peeled and diced
1 double handful quinoa
1 white onion, diced
1 thumb-length nub fresh ginger root, finely grated
9 garlic cloves, finely diced
1 double handful coconut milk
juice of 1 lemon

From the store cupboard
healing water (see p. 25)
olive oil
sea salt

Note: 2 double handfuls liquid equals 250 ml, 8 fl oz and 1 cup

To enhance the white aura of the eighth chakra, and to look and feel holy, we serve this all-white dish. When the aura is weak, your electromagnetic shield is unable to filter out the negative influences that you encounter during your day. So, protect yourself by strengthening this chakra through kriyas, meditation and good food – this dish is perfect.

- Place the diced kohlrabi and parsnip in a bamboo steamer over a saucepan of simmering water. Steam until tender.
- In a separate saucepan, place the quinoa, onion, ginger and garlic (save 1 finely diced garlic clove for the sauce). Add 1 double handful healing water and bring to the boil. Reduce the heat to low. Add 3 swirls of olive oil and 1 small gyan pinch of sea salt.
- Simmer uncovered until all the liquid is absorbed and the quinoa opens up. This will take 10–15 minutes.
- Serve topped with the Coconut Sauce (see below).
- **For the Coconut Sauce:** place the coconut milk, lemon juice and 1 finely diced garlic clove in a small saucepan over a medium heat. Stir using a circular motion until you get a creamy consistency. Season with sea salt.

Sat Nam

Guru sweet delight

You will need
1 handful dried apricots
1 large sweet potato (yam), peeled and diced
4 carrots, peeled and sliced
1 small butternut pumpkin, diced

From the store cupboard
healing water (see p. 25)
crushed nuts
raisins (optional)
cinnamon
honey
nut oil or ghee

The second, or sacral, chakra is about sensuality, creativity and flow. When yogis want to serve something that is sweet, feminine and healthy, which also gives maximum energy to the second chakra, we make this dish. Since this chakra is about survival, too, in this dish we use sweet potato, carrots and nuts for their strong earth qualities. Orange vegetables are also packed with pure phyto-chemicals.

- Place the apricots in a small bowl and cover with water. Soak for 2 hours.
- Add the prepared sweet potato, carrots, pumpkin and dried apricots to a bamboo steamer over a saucepan of simmering healing water.
- Steam until tender then transfer to serving bowls. Sprinkle over 1 handful of mixed crushed nuts and 1 handful of raisins (optional).
- Bring the water used to steam the vegetables to a fast boil. Lower the heat and simmer until the liquid is reduced by half.
- Whilst still simmering, add 1 swirl of honey, several drops of nut oil or a small spoonful of ghee, and a sprinkling of cinnamon. Stir until well combined.
- Remove the saucepan from the heat. Gently pour the liquid reduction over the steamed vegetables and crushed nuts.

Sat Nam

5 Mung beans and rice diet

Detox to cultivate balance and clarity

Easily digested and full of protein, you will be surprised to learn just how varied this diet can be. Although the Mung Beans and Rice Diet is traditionally followed as a 40-day cleansing diet, the dishes in this chapter are very nutritious and can be eaten at any time. We have included interesting variations to give you exciting options, whether you are on the diet or not, including cakes. If you do decide to follow this diet, you will find that the discipline required to maintain your focus will give you great mental strength and clarity, whether on a Kundalini yogic path or not.

For us, the authors, its significance is its connection with the 'self-sensory' system taught by Yogi Bhajan (see p. 160, Resources). In today's fickle, and increasingly more self-indulgent, world of new things and instant gratification, we are pulled to want more, to chase empty dreams of meaningless romance and fantasy, and to expect pleasure all the time. This is often the cause of personal dissatisfaction, disappointment and suffering.

Slow down, develop a meditative mind and learn to wait and see what comes to you. Learn to look within yourself – let your own creativity be your source of enjoyment and thrill. With this 'self-sensory' system, further developed through meditation, practising kriyas and diet, will come a new energy. It will flow from you to touch the lives of everyone around you, spreading your grace, compassion and nobility, creating a consciousness for the Aquarian Age (see pp. 13–17).

Mung beans and rice are not staple foods for many of us, and keeping to this diet for 40 days requires great commitment. Remember, however, that of the seven steps to happiness, commitment is the first step and is character building. So, embrace this diet with an open heart.

SPROUTING MUNG BEANS

Here we offer three ways to sprout mung beans. Each option requires you to soak the mung beans overnight.

The first option involves putting the soaked beans in a large container, in a dark place. Cover the container with a wet tea towel; wash and rinse the mung beans daily. After three days you will have fresh baby sprouts.

The second way to sprout mung beans is to place the soaked mung beans in an empty, clean jar. Cover the opening of the jar with a piece of white muslin (cheesecloth) and secure. Place the jar upside down, tilted at a slight angle, on a dish rack in a dark place. Fill the jar with water once a day, then slowly drain the water out through the muslin. After three days you should see baby sprouts. If you want larger sprouted beans, wait for one more day.

The third method is to keep the soaked beans in either a sprouting bag or a large pocket made out of muslin. Hang the bag in a dry, dark place over a container, which is required to catch the draining water. Wash the bag daily, and leave it to hang for three days.

Yogi Bhajan's mung beans, rice and vegetables

You will need

- 1 double handful white basmati rice, rinsed
- 1 double handful mung beans, rinsed
- 3 handfuls carrots, chopped
- 3 handfuls broccoli florets, chopped
- 1 large onion, diced
- 9 garlic cloves, crushed
- 1 thumb-length nub fresh ginger root, grated

From the store cupboard

- healing water (see p. 25)
- vegetable oil
- dried basil
- turmeric
- yogic spice or garam masala (see p. 27)
- red chilli flakes
- ground black pepper
- cardamom pods
- bay leaves
- tamari soy sauce

Note: 2 double handfuls liquid equals 250 ml, 8 fl oz or 1 cup

This is a classic Yogi Bhajan mung beans and rice dish that is very like a thick soup, with the vegetables and mung beans blended within the rice.

When you chant, the ultimate state of mind is the *Anahat* – the unstruck sound or vibration. In this state you are joyful, peaceful, truthful, compassionate and relaxed. Silence, is also filled with *Anahat*, and in this silence you can feel, hear and act on the call of your soul. For this recipe, remain in silent awareness throughout the preparation and cooking time, and rejoice in the *Anahat*.

- Place the rinsed basmati rice and mung beans in a large saucepan. Fill the saucepan with 9 double handfuls of healing water. Cover, bring the water to the boil, and cook over a low heat for 15 minutes. Add the carrots and broccoli, and cook for a further 11 minutes.
- Meanwhile, in a frying pan heat 2 swirls of vegetable oil. Add the onion, garlic and ginger.
- Add 3 mudra pinches of dried basil, 1 generous mudra pinch each of turmeric, yogic spice (or garam masala) and red chilli flakes, 1 small gyan pinch of ground black pepper, 4 cardamom pods and 2 bay leaves.
- Stir, tracing the outline of the infinity symbol, adding a few drops of water if required to avoid burning.
- After 4 minutes add the cooked mung beans and rice. Season with tamari.
- Keep simmering the ingredients for a further 31 minutes, or until the mixture has a thick soup consistency, the rice has virtually dissolved and the beans are tender. At this stage you may need to add more healing water.

Sat Nam

Ong so hung vegetables, sprouted beans and rice

You will need
1 beetroot
1 small red hot chilli
4 carrots
1 sweet potato (yam)
1 yellow pepper (bell)
8 broccoli florets
1 purple onion
2 double handfuls freshly sprouted beans
2 double handfuls white basmati rice
1 handful fresh parsley, chopped
1 handful fresh coriander (cilantro), chopped

From the store cupboard
olive oil
cardamom pods
healing water (see p. 25)
tamari soy sauce
sesame seeds

This is a very light, healthy and tasty mung beans and rice 'fast' food dish. You will need a bamboo steamer that is about the same size as your meal. So, if you are cooking for a large crowd, you need a large steamer! For this quick dish, we suggest you chant the heart-opening and empowering mantra *Ong So Hung* (Creator, I am Thou!) whilst cooking.

- Cut the vegetables into small cubes and place them in a bamboo steamer sitting over simmering water. As you chop the vegetables, chant *Ong So Hung.* Steam until tender, but firm to touch. Set aside.
- Wash and drain the basmati rice. Place in a pan with 1 swirl of olive oil and 2 cardamom pods.
- Cover the rice with healing water. Cook on a low heat until the water is absorbed and the rice is soft. For added flavour, you can use the water from under the steamed vegetables.
- Once the rice is ready, add the steamed vegetables and mix well. Add the chopped parsley and coriander, then season with tamari.
- Just before serving toss through the freshly sprouted beans, and garnish with a generous sprinkling of sesame seeds.

Sat Nam

Summer ong mung beans and rice

You will need
1 double handful brown basmati rice
1 leek, sliced
7 garlic cloves, finely chopped
1 large purple onion
4 courgettes (zucchini), diced
4 tomatoes, diced
1 red pepper (sweet), diced
1 double handful sprouted mung beans
1 mudra pinch chopped fresh basil (for garnish)
1 mudra pinch chopped fresh mint (for garnish)

From the store cupboard
cumin seeds
coriander seeds
mustard seeds
red hot chilli flakes
healing water (see p. 25)
tamari soy sauce
olive oil

This is a great summer-cleansing dish where we combine fresh summer vegetables such as courgettes, tomatoes and red pepper with fresh green herbs.

- Rinse the rice well. Set aside.
- In a saucepan over a medium heat, dry-sauté the leek, garlic and onion with a few drops of water. Add 1 mudra pinch each of the cumin seeds, coriander seeds, mustard seeds and the chilli flakes. Stir well in a circular motion, adding a few drops of water, as required.
- Add the prepared courgettes, tomatoes and red pepper. Stir a few more times, then add the rinsed rice and sprouted mung beans. Cover with healing water and bring to the boil. Lower the heat and simmer until the rice is cooked.
- For flavour, add 1 swirl of both tamari and olive oil.
- Serve garnished with chopped fresh basil and mint.

Sat Nam

Winter so hung mung beans and rice

You will need
1 double handful brown basmati rice
1 medium onion, diced
7 garlic cloves, crushed
1 thumb-length nub fresh ginger root, grated
1 double handful sprouted mung beans
1 sweet potato (yam), peeled and cubed
4 carrots, cubed
1 beetroot (beet), cubed
1 small butternut squash (pumpkin), cubed
7 florets broccoli

The mung bean and rice diet is perfect for winter cleansing. This recipe is the super-winter-cleansing dish. It includes root vegetables, which are warming, and the trinity roots, which are both warming and grounding. When you talk about grounding, you refer to the base, or root, chakra (energy centre). This chakra is about foundation, security and habit.

We all need to develop a basic instinct of trust, because a lack of trust stops the energies flowing from the base chakra into the higher chakras. Grounding foods help this flow of energy. As Guru Nanak said in the *Japji*, 'Why do we worry? When the flamingo flies away, God takes care of its young.' *Japji* is the first message that sprang from Guru Nanak's lips, like nectar, as he emerged from the river after three days. It is said that it takes three days for the ego to totally disappear – it is then that one experiences the Ultimate.

- Rinse the rice well. Set aside.
- In a saucepan, sauté over a medium heat for 3 minutes the onion, garlic (1 clove for each chakra) and ginger. You can dry-sauté, adding a few drops of water as needed, or sauté using a few swirls of vegetable oil. Add the sprouted mung beans and the rice.
- Mix, then add 1 mudra pinch each of fennel seeds and cayenne pepper, 2 mudra pinches cumin powder and 3 cardamom pods. If you enjoy a really spicy taste, add more spices.

From the store cupboard
vegetable oil
fennel seeds
cayenne pepper
cumin powder
cardamom pods
healing water (see p. 25)
olive oil
tamari soy sauce

- Mix using a circular motion for a few moments, then add enough healing water to cover all the ingredients.
- Cover the saucepan and reduce the heat to low. Cook the mixture until the rice is soft. This will take between 11 and 22 minutes.
- While the mung beans and rice are cooking, steam the sweet potato, carrots, beetroot and butternut squash in a bamboo steamer – these vegetables are all for grounding and balancing the lower triangle chakras. Add the broccoli florets, for the heart chakra.
- Once the vegetables are soft, but still firm to the touch, add the rice and mung beans. Mix well, tracing the outline of the infinity symbol, as you stir.
- Before serving add 1 swirl each of olive oil and tamari for both taste and fragrance.
- This dish can be served hot, or it can be reheated up to 2 days after it's made.

Sat Nam

Winter so hung mung bean and rice

Sprouted happy mung bean salad

You will need
1 handful sprouted mung beans
1 iceberg lettuce, sliced
2 celery sticks (stalks), sliced
2 large tomatoes, chopped
2 carrots, shredded
1 handful basil, roughly chopped
1 handful mint, roughly chopped
1 handful parsley, roughly chopped
1 thumb-length nub fresh ginger root, grated
juice of 1 large lemon

From the store cupboard
chilli flakes
balsamic or apple vinegar
olive oil
tamari soy sauce
sea salt

(serves 2 people)

Sprouted mung beans are living foods, full of goodness that is so easily destroyed by cooking. By sprouting beans we are activating them, releasing the full nutritional value of the tender young shoots. They taste absolutely wonderful, and when used in a hot dish, require less preparation and cooking than dried mung beans.

- Toss together the freshly sprouted mung beans, lettuce, celery, tomatoes, shredded carrots and fresh herbs, plus a sprinkle of chilli flakes.
- Add the ginger and lemon juice. Toss through.
- Dress with a few drops of vinegar, 4 swirls of olive oil and 1 swirl of tamari. Season with sea salt.
- Mix with happiness whilst chanting the *Guru* mantra (see p. 155).

Sat Nam

Yogi Bhajan's classic trinity rice

You will need
2 double handfuls white basmati rice
2 large onions, chopped
2 garlic cloves, sliced
1 thumb-length nub fresh ginger root, grated
1 large tomato, peeled and chopped
8–10 handfuls chopped vegetables, assorted

From the store cupboard
ghee
tamari soy sauce
healing water (see p. 25)

Note: 2 double handfuls liquid equals 250 ml, 8 fl oz or 1 cup

This is a very cleansing and nourishing dish that can be eaten either on its own or with a fresh salad of mung beans. Once it is made, you can keep it in the refrigerator to be eaten cold, although the sooner it is eaten the more nutritious it will be.

For this dish, we recommend you chant the *Guru* mantra (see p. 155). This mantra balances the energies concerned with the principles of generating, organising and transforming, and expresses ecstasy through knowledge and experience.

- Rinse the rice thoroughly and set aside.
- Heat a saucepan over a medium heat. Add ½ cup (125 gm/4 oz) of ghee and melt.
- Add the onions, garlic and ginger to the melted ghee. Mix until these 'trinity roots' are very soft, then add the rice.
- Add the chopped tomato and assorted vegetables. Mix well and drizzle over 4 rounds of tamari.
- Cover the ingredients with 8 double handfuls of healing water, turn the heat down to low, and cook until the rice and vegetables are tender.

Sat Nam

Italian guru's risotto

You will need
2 double handfuls risotto rice
4 garlic cloves, crushed
1 onion, diced
1 leek, sliced
4 carrots, sliced
4 tomatoes, diced
1 broccoli head, cut in florets
2 handfuls white mushrooms, chopped
fresh basil leaves (for garnish)

From the store cupboard
dried basil
Herbes de Provence
bay leaves
yogic or organic stock (bouillon) cubes (see p. 27)
healing water (see p. 25)
olive oil
sea salt
balsamic vinegar

This version of mung beans and rice holds the flavours of the Mediterranean; it is a lovely alternative to the more traditional Indian influences in yogic foods.

- Wash the risotto rice thoroughly. Set aside.
- In a large saucepan, dry-sauté the garlic, onion and leek in a few drops of water.
- Add 1 mudra pinch each of dried basil and Herbes de Provence and 2 bay leaves. Mix well before adding 2 stock cubes, crumbled between your fingers.
- Add to the saucepan the prepared carrots, tomatoes, broccoli florets and mushrooms. Mix well, then add the rice.
- Next, slowly add small amounts of healing water. Stir continuously, tracing the outline of the infinity symbol, allowing the water to be completely absorbed before adding the next handful. Continue this process until the rice is tender.
- Add 3 swirls of olive oil, and stir through. Season with sea salt and balsamic vinegar.
- Garnish with roughly chopped fresh basil leaves and serve.

Sat Nam

Rice noodles and guru's vegetables

You will need
1 onion, diced
7 garlic cloves, crushed
1 thumb-length nub ginger root, grated
3 lime leaves (fresh or dried)
1 small stick lemon grass, finely sliced
1 red chilli, chopped
4 carrots, sliced
4 courgettes (zucchini), diced
1 small sweet potato (yam), diced
1 can (400ml/14 fl oz) coconut milk
2 handfuls (250 g/9 oz) rice noodles
2 handfuls baby spinach
fresh coriander leaves (cilantro), roughly chopped

From the store cupboard
olive oil
healing water (see p. 25)
tamari soy sauce
crushed peanuts
sesame oil

This is a popular, festival dish with a Thai twist. Try it with thick noodles, as these soak up the delicious spicy coconut juices.

While cooking this dish we suggest you chant *Guroo Guroo Wha-hay Guroo, Guroo Raam Daas Guroo*. Guru Ram Das was the fourth Sikh Guru, and Kundalini Yoga descends from the House of Guru Ram Das. This is the lineage of Kundalini Yogis, as Yogi Bhajan accepted Guru Ram Das as his teacher.

- In a large frying pan, sauté the onion, garlic, ginger, lime leaves and lemon grass until aromatic and well combined.
- Add 3 swirls of olive oil and the fresh chilli, and mix thoroughly.
- Add the carrots, courgettes and sweet potato. Sauté for a few moments, tracing the outline of a triangle, as you stir.
- Next, add the coconut milk and enough healing water to cover the vegetables. Bring to the boil, then reduce the heat and simmer until the vegetables are tender.
- Whilst the vegetables are cooking, prepare the rice noodles. Fill a large saucepan with water and bring to the boil. Immerse the noodles into the water, then turn down the heat. Cook according to the packet instructions.
- Once the noodles are al dente, drain and add them to the simmering stew, a few at a time, to ensure the noodles and the vegetables are thoroughly coated in the coconut sauce.
- Add the baby spinach, mix once, then season with tamari, to taste.
- Garnish with crushed peanuts and fresh coriander. Drizzle over a few drops of sesame oil for added flavour.

Sat Nam

Solstice mung beans and rice (the solstice diet)

You will need
1 double handful mung beans, rinsed
1 double handful white basmati rice, rinsed
1 large onion, diced
9 garlic cloves, crushed
2 thumb-length nubs fresh ginger root, grated
1 small iceberg lettuce
Soltice Hot Sauce (see p. 72)

From the store cupboard
healing water (see p. 25)
vegetable oil
turmeric
red chilli flakes
sea salt

Solstice Diet: Breakfast
2 oranges
2 bananas
Solstice Morning Soup (see p. 72)

Dinner
Solstice Mung Beans and rice (see right)
Solstice Hot Sauce (see p. 72)
Steamed sliced carrot and beetroot (beet)

(pictured on page 73)

This recipe is part of the famous Solstice Diet, given by Yogi Bhajan for the key winter and summer solstice festivals that take place in the USA and France. Yogi Bhajan recommended you stick to the diet for 10 days and that, during this period, you practise the *'Awakening the Inner Healer*: a healing *sadhana* to initiate the healing zone in you' (originally taught by Yogi Bhajan in November 1985).

This is a diet that increases the alkalinity of the blood. Since the average diet of most people includes foods that are acid-producing (items such as sugar, dairy and coffee) increasing alkalinity is important for maintaining a balanced system. If our blood acidity–alkalinity is not balanced, our bodies inefficiently utilise the enzymes in the foods we eat, and do not properly absorb the trace nutrients, vitamins, minerals and fatty acids.

The Solstice Diet is high in fibre and is very cleansing – it also brings about a meditative mind. During this diet drink plenty of healing water (see p. 25), purified water or mineral water. An outline of the diet can be found on the left-hand side of this page, below the ingredients used to make this particular dish.

This Solstice Mung Beans and Rice dish, as provided by Yogi Bhajan, is served for dinner when you are on the Solstice Diet. It is eaten as the main meal of the day, since lunch is not eaten unless you are on this diet during the Tantric Days, you are a child or a pregnant woman.

- Place the rinsed mung beans and basmati rice in a large saucepan. Fill the saucepan with 7 double handfuls of healing water. Cover, bring the water to the boil, and cook over a low heat for 15 minutes. Do not drain.
- Meanwhile, in a frying pan heat 2 swirls of vegetable oil. Add the onion, garlic and ginger.
- Add 1 generous mudra pinch each of turmeric and red chilli flakes.
- Stir, tracing the outline of the infinity symbol, adding a few drops of water if required to avoid burning.
- After 4 minutes add the cooked mung beans and rice, including the liquid. Season with sea salt.
- Simmer the ingredients for a further 31 minutes, or until the mixture has a thick soup consistency, the rice has virtually dissolved and the beans are tender. At this stage you may need to add more healing water.
- Once cooked, spoon the beans and rice on to a plate and ladle over a generous serving of Solstice Hot Sauce (see p. 72)
- Serve with whole iceberg lettuce leaves that can be used to scoop up the Solstice Mung Beans and Rice.

Sat Nam

Solstice hot sauce

You will need
3 large onions, chopped
1 double handful tamarind concentrate
2–3 double handfuls sesame oil
2 double handfuls apple cider vinegar
10 small whole dried red chillies
9 mudra pinches dried red chilli flakes

From the store cupboard
healing water (see p. 25)
turmeric

Note: 2 double handfuls liquid equals 250 ml, 8 fl oz or 1 cup

The Solstice Hot Sauce is an extremely spicy treat for any dish or meal. Of native Mexican origin, it was adopted for the Kundalini Yoga summer and winter solstice. The longer you keep the sauce in the refrigerator, allowing the flavours to mature, the better it will taste – this is why we recommend it be left for at least two days.

- Put the chopped onions in a large glass bowl and sprinkle with 9 mudra pinches of dried red chilli flakes.
- Dissolve the tamarind concentrate in 2 double handfuls of healing water. Add to the chopped onion and chilli mix and the sesame oil. Mix well.
- Sprinkle over 3 mudra pinches of turmeric, then add the apple cider vinegar and the whole red chillies.
- Stir well, tracing the outline of the infinity symbol, whilst chanting *Har-Har*.
- Let the sauce sit in the refrigerator for a minimum of 1 night before using it.

Sat Nam

Solstice morning soup

You will need
2 potatoes
1 whole celery
1 onion
2 large garlic cloves, crushed
1 banana, sliced (optional)

From the store cupboard
healing water (see p. 25)
tamari soy sauce
olive oil
chilli powder
turmeric
ground cumin
ground coriander
cayenne pepper

This soup promotes blood alkalinity and mental balance, and is served for breakfast when on the Solstice Diet. To counter-balance the spiciness, you may wish to add one sliced banana.

In remembrance of Yogi Bhajan's graceful presence at the solstice celebrations, we suggest a beautiful chant to accompany this dish is the *Akal, Maha, Kal* (Undying, Great Death) – it is powerful, life-giving and helps to remove fear and relax the mind.

- Slice the potatoes and dice the celery and onion – you should end up with equal quantities of each vegetable, so add more if required.
- Place the potatoes in a saucepan. Top with the diced celery and onion, and enough healing water to cover all the vegetables.
- Sprinkle with a few drops of tamari, then simmer until the vegetables are tender.
- In the meantime, sauté 2 swirls of olive oil, 6 mudra pinches of chilli powder, 3 mudra pinches each of turmeric, ground cumin and ground coriander, and 1 pinch of cayenne pepper over a low heat. Be careful to make sure the spices do not burn, but are heated just enough to release their full flavours and aromas.
- Mix the sautéed spices through the soup when the vegetables are tender.
- Add the crushed garlic just before serving, and serve with 1 sliced banana to counter-balance the spiciness (optional).
- For convenience, this soup can be prepared the night before and reheated the following morning.

Sat Nam

TOP Solstice morning soup
CENTRE Solstice hot sauce
ABOVE Solstice mung beans and rice (see p. 71)

Mung beans sat curry

You will need
2 handfuls mung beans
1 onion, diced
7 garlic cloves, crushed
4 carrots, diced
4 medium potatoes, diced
4 generous handfuls baby spinach

From the store cupboard
healing water (see p. 25)
vegetable oil
yogic spice or garam masala (see p. 27)
curry powder
cayenne pepper
turmeric
mustard seeds
yogic or organic stock (bouillon) cube (see p. 27)
tamari soy sauce

This is a great example of yogic fast food. When cooking for a large number of people, simply allow one handful of mung beans for every two people. It is a masculine dish, a conqueror of evil, and the mantra for this dish is *Har Singh Nar Singh* (see p. 155).

- Soak the mung beans overnight in plenty of water. Drain and rinse.
- Add the soaked mung beans to a saucepan filled with plenty of water. Cook until the beans are soft – this will take approximately1½ hours. Drain again and set aside.
- Dry-sauté in a saucepan the onion and garlic with a few drops of water.
- Add 2 swirls of vegetable oil and 3 mudra pinches each of yogic spice (or garam masala), curry powder, cayenne pepper, turmeric and mustard seeds. Combine well, stirring using a circular motion.
- Add the carrots and potatoes and toss through until they are thoroughly coated with the spices. Add 2 stock cubes and enough healing water to completely cover the vegetables. Simmer until the vegetables are tender.
- Once the vegetables are ready, add to the pan the cooked mung beans and the baby spinach. Continue to simmer over a low heat until the flavours are well dispersed throughout the dish, and it is heated through.
- Season with tamari, if desired, and serve.

Sat Nam

Mung beans nam dhal

You will need
2 handfuls mung beans
4 garlic cloves, crushed
1 thumb-length nub fresh ginger root, grated
1 medium purple onion, diced
fresh basil leaves (for garnish)

From the store cupboard
olive oil
yogic spice or garam masala (see p. 27)
ground cumin
oregano
turmeric
ground black pepper
cayenne pepper
healing water (see p. 25)
tamari soy sauce

This dhal goes very well with rice, vegetables and salads. Dhal can be made using a variety of beans and lentils – for this dish we created a recipe using mung beans. Whilst the dish is simmering away chant the mantra *Jap Man Sat Nam* (see p. 155). This mantra opens you to the flow of prosperity by attuning the mind to the power of *Har*, the creative Infinity and the joy of merging with Infinity.

- Soak the mung beans overnight in plenty of water. Drain.
- Heat a saucepan over a medium heat. Add 3 swirls of olive oil (1 for each of the 3 levels of our being), the garlic, fresh ginger and diced purple onion.
- Mix well, tracing the outline of the infinity symbol, as you stir. Add 1 large pinch each of the yogic spice (or garam masala), cumin, oregano, turmeric, ground black pepper and 1 gyan pinch of cayenne pepper. Increase or decrease the amount of cayenne pepper according to how 'hot' you want the dish to be. Mix well before adding the drained mung beans.
- Cover with healing water. Bring to the boil, then lower the heat and simmer until the beans are soft and the liquid takes on a thick consistency – approximately 1½ hours.
- Season with tamari and serve garnished with a sprinkling of chopped fresh basil leaves.

Sat Nam

Mung beans light salad with sesame sauce

You will need
2 handfuls mung beans
1 medium purple onion, diced
1 large tomato, diced
1 carrot, diced
1 mudra pinch chopped fresh mint
1 handful baby spinach
juice of half a lemon

From the store cupboard
olive oil
organic tahini paste
healing water (see p. 25)
tamari soy sauce
sesame seeds

This salad can be eaten either warm or cold, as a side dish or as a main course. It is a popular salad in many African countries. Here, we present it with a yogic twist.

- Soak the mung beans in plenty of water overnight. Drain.
- Cook the soaked mung beans in a large saucepan of water until al dente. This will take approximately 1 hour. It is important for the flavour of the dish that they are not over-cooked.
- In a frying pan, sauté the diced purple onion with 1 swirl of olive oil until golden in colour and soft. Toss through the diced tomato and carrot, for the lower chakras, and the cooked mung beans. Add a generous sprinkling of fresh mint leaves and the baby spinach, for the heart centre.
- Mix well, then drizzle over the Sesame Sauce (see below) and a sprinkling of lightly toasted sesame seeds. Serve either warm or cold.
- **For the Sesame Sauce:** add equal quantities of tahini paste and healing water to a small glass bowl. We recommend 3 spoonfuls of each. Mix well, then add the juice of half a lemon. If it is too thin or watery, add more tahini paste. Season with a few drops of tamari and set aside.

Sat Nam

Divine basmati rice with herbs

You will need
2 handfuls white basmati rice
1 white onion, diced
1 purple onion, diced
4 garlic cloves, crushed
2 generous handfuls baby spinach
1 handful fresh basil, chopped
1 handful fresh mint, chopped
1 handful fresh parsley, chopped
mixed fresh herbs (for garnish)

From the store cupboard
yogic or organic stock (bouillon) cube (see p. 27)
healing water (see p. 25)
sea salt
olive oil

Breathing is a very important component of Kundalini Yoga. Yogi Bhajan called it the 'tender charge of the Divine'. Whilst the rice is cooking, use the opportunity to practise the *Breath of Fire* (see p. 30), which is a powerful, cleansing breath. It also re-magnetises the cells, insulating you from the effects of electromagnetic pollution.

- Thoroughly rinse the basmati rice under running water.
- Dry-sauté the white and purple onions in a frying pan, adding a few drops of water as needed to prevent burning.
- Once the onions are soft, add the garlic. Continue to stir until the aroma of the garlic permeates the onions. Add the rice and stir, tracing the outline of a triangle, to combine.
- Crumble over the stock cube, then pour over enough healing water to cover the rice.
- Add the baby spinach, fresh basil, mint and parsley. Simmer over a low heat until all the liquid is completely absorbed by the rice. Season with sea salt.
- To serve, garnish with a sprinkling of finely chopped mixed herbs and a drizzle of olive oil. The gentle Mediterranean flavours of this dish go well with steamed vegetables, a fresh green salad or sprouted mung beans.

Sat Nam

Gobind rice, seeds and vegetables

You will need
1 double handful mung beans
2 double handfuls white basmati rice,
2 toasted nori sheets, shredded
1 avocado, diced
1 thumb-nail nub fresh ginger root, grated

From the store cupboard
healing water (see p. 25)
sesame seeds
pumpkin seeds
sunflower seeds
tamari soy sauce
sesame oil

This dish is reminiscent of Japanese sushi, but without the fiddly preparation. It does not compromise on the taste, though, as each mouthful is bursting with flavour and crunch from the abundant use of seeds.

As you eat it you will enjoy the unusual sensation of the crunchy rice mixture and the soft avocado. In a similar way, Guru Gobind Singh was an unusual man. Apart from being a warrior, he was also a renowned poet. In 1684, he wrote the *Var Sri Bhagauti Ji Ki*, popularly called *Chandi di Var*. The poem was about the contest between the gods and the demons. The choice of a warlike theme was to infuse martial spirit among his followers, and prepare them to stand up against injustice and tyranny.

- Soak the mung beans overnight in plenty of water. Drain, then place in a saucepan and cook in healing water. Cook until al dente.
- Rinse the basmati rice thoroughly. Set aside.
- Place the semi-cooked beans and the rinsed rice in a large saucepan with 1 handful each of sesame, pumpkin and sunflower seeds.
- Sauté over a medium heat for a few moments, then add enough healing water to completely cover all the ingredients. Bring to the boil.
- Add 2 swirls of tamari and the shredded nori sheets. Lower the heat, cover and simmer for 11 minutes or until all the water is absorbed by the rice. Transfer to a serving platter.
- Sprinkle over the diced avocado and grated ginger. Drizzle with sesame oil and serve.

Sat Nam

Rice and mung beans ma pudding

You will need
1 double handful mung beans
1 double handful white basmati rice
8 pitted dates, diced
2 thumb-nail nubs fresh ginger root, grated
1 small apple, grated

From the store cupboard
coconut or rice milk
cardamom pod
honey
sesame seeds

This sweet dish is unlike any other mung beans and rice dish. You can use either rice milk or coconut milk, and if you prefer a less creamy taste, you can also substitute the milk with healing water. It is very nurturing, and is a reflection of Yogi Bhajan's celebration of womanhood. He once said that there are only four powers on the Earth: the power of prayer; the power of prayer of the mother; the power of prayer of the beloved; and the power of prayer of a noble woman.

- Soak the mung beans overnight in plenty of water. Drain.
- Place the basmati rice and mung beans in a pan, covering with an equal amount of coconut milk or rice milk to rice and beans – approximately 250 ml/8 fl oz/1 cup.
- Add the dates, for the aura, the ginger, 1 cardamom pod and 4 swirls of honey. Simmer over a low heat for 22–31 minutes, or until all the liquid is absorbed into the rice.
- Before serving, garnish with the shredded apple and a sprinkling of sesame seeds.

Sat Nam

Rice ra mung beans and honey steamer cake

You will need
1 double handful sushi rice
1 double handful mung beans
4 mudra pinches raw sugar
4 spoonfuls honey
1 thumb-length nub fresh ginger, grated
Yogic Dessert Cream (see p. 119) (optional)
jam (optional)

This is the yogic version of a traditional Japanese pudding, which is served in delicate individual portions in little bamboo steamers. We use very simple ingredients and a simple method to prepare it. Let the cake steam for 62 minutes. Knowing a treat awaits you, do your favourite 62-minute meditation whilst the cake is cooking.

- Soak overnight the rice and mung beans in 2 separate bowls. Drain and rinse well.
- Boil the mung beans in water for 11 minutes.
- Put the soaked rice into a food processor and grind to a paste. Add the sugar (this gives a subtle, sweet taste to the cake). Set aside.
- Drain the boiled mung beans and process in a food processor until you get a paste. Add 4 generous swirls of honey (approximately 4 spoonfuls) and the grated ginger.
- Take a bamboo steamer (20 cm/8 in) and line the base with a thin muslin cloth (cheesecloth). Fold in the corners so that the cloth lies flat.
- Spread half the bean paste over the base of the steamer. Next, spread over the sticky rice paste, then finish with a layer of the remaining bean paste. Press each layer down firmly or the cake will fall apart when removed from the steamer after it is cooked.
- Place the steamer over a saucepan of simmering water. Cook for 62 minutes.
- Serve hot with Yogic Dessert Cream (see p. 119) or cold as a snack topped with jam.
- This cake will keep well in the refrigerator for 1 day. It is also suitable for freezing.

Sat Nam

Sesame sa seed honey spread with rice cakes

You will need
1 jar (330 ml/11½ fl oz) tahini paste
honey, to taste
healing water (see p. 25)
unsalted organic rice cakes
fresh mint leaves (for garnish)
sliced fresh fruit (for garnish)

Halva is one of the most favoured sweets from the Middle East; this is our 'healthy' version. In this recipe, the traditional flavours come from the sauce that you spread over the rice cakes. To cut down on the intake of processed food, which depletes *prana*, we have replaced the sugar with honey.

This delicious snack is easy to make and is very nutritious, too. Sesame seeds are packed with protein, iron, calcium and magnesium.

- Spoon the tahini paste into a large bowl and beat very rapidly in a circular motion.
- Drizzle over a few spoonfuls of honey. Blend with the tahini until it is completely dissolved. Taste, adding more honey, if desired. For a thinner consistency, add a few drops of healing water as you mix.
- To serve, spread the rice cakes with a generous amount of the Sesame Sa Seed Honey. Garnish each rice cake with a sprig of fresh mint and a few slices of fresh fruit such as kiwi fruit or banana.

Sat Nam

Guru's fruit and nut muesli (see p. 82)

6 Fruit, nuts and vegetables

Cleanse and rebuild your body

Fruit, nuts and vegetables are central to the day-to-day diet of all yogis. As they are a rich source of fibre, vitamins and minerals, they are also the cornerstone to good health. Many vegetables, especially the green, leafy and juicy varieties, have the effect of alkalising the blood, and by doing so, bring about equilibrium. Many of the foods we eat, such as sugars, fats, coffee and processed food, acidify our blood; maintaining an optimal acid-alkaline balance is key to good health.

Another benefit of following the Fruit, Nut and Vegetable Diet is that nuts are a rich source of protein, essential oils and fibre. Also, a diet that consists solely of fruit, nuts and vegetables helps with the elimination process, due to the high fibre content. When our insides are moving smoothly, fewer waste materials are stored in the colon, which means fewer toxins are re-absorbed back into the bloodstream.

Over-cooking destroys the natural goodness of fruit and vegetables. In our recipes, therefore, when cooking is required, we advocate 'light cooking'. Raw or lightly cooked, they taste wonderful. You will also find you need very little in terms of seasoning to make them taste good.

In addition to recipes for a general Fruit, Nut and Vegetable Diet, in this chapter we present a number of specific Kundalini Yoga diet paths – the Fruit Fast, the Banana Fast and the Melon Diet. These, however, are suitable only for people who already have some experience of fasting. A good idea is to follow a diet such as the Mung Beans and Rice Diet for 40 days, first.

Guru's fruit and nut muesli

You will need
2 apples, cored and grated
1 finger-length nub fresh ginger root, finely grated
1–2 handfuls desiccated (shredded) coconut
tahini paste
1 spoonful honey
1 handful raisins
1 handful mixed nuts, chopped
ground cinnamon

Serves 2 people

(pictured on page 80)

This muesli provides a wonderful start to the day. You can use any combination of dried and fresh fruit and berries, just as long as you always include the apples, coconut and ginger, which are its foundation. Whilst you prepare this muesli for breakfast, start your day by singing the *Laya Yoga Kundalini* mantra for seven minutes (see p. 155). This mantra is traditionally chanted at morning *sadhana* without musical instruments. When chanted, it activates the kundalini energy at the base of your spine, initiating the relationship between your soul and the universal soul.

- Grate the apples and ginger, dividing evenly between 2 bowls.
- Add to each bowl a half portion of the desiccated coconut, 1 spoonful of tahini and 1 spoonful of honey, or to taste.
- Divide the raisins and chopped nuts between the two bowls, scattering them over the top. For added flavour, sprinkle with cinnamon.

Sat Nam

Corn sa porridge and fruit

You will need
2 double handfuls organic polenta
healing water (see p. 25)
1 yogic or organic stock (bouillon) cube (see p. 27)
1 cardamom pod
1 star anise
2 double handfuls berries and fruit, any combination
honey

Not only is this dish a delightful breakfast treat, it is also a lovely dessert, complementing any meal of fresh salad and nuts, or a vegetable dish.

A mantra suitable for the morning, because it is full of bright energy, is *Waah Yantee, Kaar Yantee* (see p. 155). Bring this energy into your day by chanting it whilst preparing your breakfast. The words come directly from the sage Patanjali, who systemised the study of yoga. Therefore this dish encapsulates thousands of years of prayer.

- Place a large saucepan over a medium heat. Pour in the polenta and mix in a circular motion for a few moments. Note the level of the polenta in the pan for later when you will need 4 parts water to 1 part polenta.
- Once the polenta turns to a light brown, remove the saucepan from the heat and transfer the contents to another container. Set aside.
- Using the same saucepan, add the healing water (see above).
- Add the stock cube, lower the heat and stir. When the cube has dissolved, slowly pour in the polenta. Keep stirring, chanting as you do so.
- Remove the seeds from the cardamom pod and add them to the polenta along with the star anise. Combine well, allowing the wonderful flavours to seep through the entire dish.
- Add the berries and fruit just before serving.
- Sweeten with honey, to taste.

Sat Nam

Rejuvenating ma fruit salad

You will need
All variations
1 handful fresh mint
1 handful tarragon
1 finger-length nub fresh ginger root, grated
honey

Version one: semi-sweet
2 handfuls mixed berries
1 pineapple, diced
2 oranges, cut into segments
pulp of 1 passionfruit

Version two: Sweet
1 papaya, diced
1 mango, diced
1 pear, diced
1 peach, diced
2 kiwis, diced
1 apple, shredded
1 handful grapes

Version three: extra sweet
4 fresh figs, cut into segments
2 bananas, sliced
8 fresh dates, chopped
1 handful mixed dried fruit
healing water (see p. 25)

In this recipe we use three different groups of fruit to make three different fruit salads – the thread linking all three together is the use of ginger, mint, tarragon and honey. Serve each on its own as an entire meal, or as an entrée or dessert – leave a gap of one hour before or after the main dish before eating these salads.

This is a beautiful dish to share with friends, and in Kundalini Yoga, the sharing of food goes beyond the social element – it is part of its heritage – bringing people together to practise yoga so that the energies of the entire group are merged into one. People begin to communicate on the same wavelength, creating group consciousness. Simply by tuning in with a *Sat Naam*, if you do not intend to do *sadhana*, is OK, too.

- For each version, place the prepared fruit in a bowl, and toss together with your hands.
- Roughly chop the fresh mint and tarragon, and grate the ginger.
- Add the mint, tarragon and ginger to the fruit and mix well.
- Sweeten to taste with honey.
- Chant a long *Maaaa* to bring the sun energy into the salad and serve.
- For the Extra Sweet Version, soften the mixed dried fruit by soaking it in an equal quantity of healing water to fruit for at least 62 minutes – they are even better when soaked overnight. Add both the fruit and any juices not absorbed by the fruit to the salad.

Sat Nam

Fruit and nut hey smoothie

You will need
1 handful raw almonds
1 handful walnuts
healing water (see p. 25)
1 handful pumpkin seeds
1 handful raisins
1 double handful blueberries
2 bananas
1 small mango, flesh only
1 thumb-length nub fresh ginger root, grated
1 cup (250 ml/8 fl oz) pineapple juice, unsweetened

This delicious smoothie, made without yoghurt, milk or cream, is a balanced meal in a glass. Its richness comes from the nuts that are soaked for 11 hours, or overnight. This process is to re-energise the nuts so that they burst with healthy enzymes. To give you an even greater boost, practise the *Kriya for Optimum Health* (see pp. 148–150).

- Soak the raw almonds and walnuts in plenty of healing water in 2 separate bowls for 11 hours.
- Drain the nuts, remove the skins from the raw almonds, and then place both the almonds and walnuts into a food processor along with all the other ingredients. If the almond skins do not come off easily, soak them again in boiling water for 10 seconds. Drain and peel.
- Blend until smooth.

Sat Nam

Beetroot and carrot ji stew with nut sauce

You will need
4 beetroots (beets), diced
5 carrots, diced
1 purple onion, diced
4 garlic cloves, crushed
parsley leaves (for garnish)

From the store cupboard
cashew nuts
macadamia nuts
olive oil
seeds from 1 cardamom pod
dried red chilli flakes
healing water (see p. 25)
sea salt

This dish is based on a classic Yogi Bhajan recipe, using a very versatile, energy-rich nut sauce as an alternative to the cheese. The use of beetroot means this stew is both tasty and a good cleanser for the liver and digestive tract. To complement this dish, do the Yogi Bhajan's *Detoxification Kriya* (see pp. 142–44).

- Soak the cashew nuts and macadamia nuts for 8 hours or overnight. These will be used in the nut sauce (see below).
- Place the beetroot and carrots in a steamer over simmering water. Steam until the vegetables are soft, but still firm to touch.
- Whilst the vegetables are steaming, sauté the purple onion with a few drops each of water and olive oil in a frying pan.
- Add the crushed garlic and the cardamom seeds. Stir, tracing the outline of the infinity symbol, until well combined. Add 1 mudra pinch of red chilli flakes.
- When the beetroot and carrot are ready, toss through the onion and spice mixture until well coated. Season with sea salt.
- To serve, spread the Nut Sauce (see below) over the serving dish. Spoon on the vegetables, and garnish with the parsley leaves.
- **For the Nut Sauce:** blend the soaked cashew and macadamia nuts in a food processor with 1 swirl of olive oil until creamy. You may need to add a little healing water to achieve a smooth consistency.

Sat Nam

Nut and chakra vegetable soup

You will need
1 handful mixed nuts
1 handful pumpkin seeds
4 potatoes, diced
4 carrots, diced
4 celery sticks (stalks), sliced
2 onions, diced
1 broccoli head, florets
4 garlic cloves
1 handful parsley leaves, roughly chopped

From the store cupboard
olive oil
healing water (see p. 25)
yogic stock or organic stock (bouillon) cubes (see p. 27)
tamari soy sauce
red chilli flakes (optional)

The strong combination of mixed nuts and vegetables makes this dish a powerhouse of energy that you can use to facilitate changes in your life. Most of your states of consciousness can be thought of as postures that affect your breathing and mind patterns – some static and some dynamic. By changing your body posture and breathing rhythm, and through vibration, you can change your state. So make sure your spine is straight, raise your heart to the skies, drop your shoulders to the earth and think kind loving thoughts.

- Soak the mixed nuts and pumpkin seeds in separate bowls for 11 hours.
- Heat a large saucepan over a medium heat. Place the prepared potatoes, carrots, celery sticks, onions, broccoli and garlic into the saucepan with 4 swirls of olive oil. Mix together, tracing the outline of the infinity symbol.
- Add enough healing water to just cover the vegetables. Add the stock cube.
- Bring the water to the boil, reduce the heat and simmer until the vegetables are tender.
- Whilst the vegetables are cooking, drain the mixed nuts and pumpkin seeds and place into a food processor. Add equal portions of healing water and olive oil until the liquid mix is level with the nuts. Blend until smooth.
- Once the vegetables are cooked, add the nut purée and parsley leaves to the simmering soup. Stir 3 times in a circular motion, then take the saucepan off the heat.
- Either blend the mixture into a creamy soup or leave it as is. Season with tamari, to taste.
- To serve, sprinkle with a small gyan pinch of chilli flakes (optional).

Sat Nam

Grilled veg with nut and seed da cream

You will need
1 handful mixed nuts
1 handful pumpkin seeds
juice of 1 lemon
1 handful fresh basil, chopped
1 handful fresh mint, chopped
1 sweet potato (yam)
1 purple onion
4 carrots
1 fennel bulb
2 courgettes (zucchini)
fresh basil leaves
4 garlic cloves
tomato juice

From the store cupboard
olive oil
tamari soy sauce
cayenne pepper
ground cumin
dried mint (optional)
dried basil (optional)

The vegetables in this dish are marinated and grilled, giving it a lovely Mediterranean accent. Whilst the vegetables marinate we recommend you do the Raa Maa Daa Saa Saa Say So Hung Healing Meditation for healing and for peace (see p. 153). The sweet potato (yam) is included for both its grounding, earth energy and its nutritional value.

- Soak the mixed nuts and pumpkin seeds, in separate bowls, for 11 hours. These will be used for the Nut and Seed Da Cream (see below).
- Prepare a marinade by thoroughly combining the juice of 1 lemon, chopped basil and mint, 4 swirls of olive oil, 18 drops of tamari, 1 small gyan pinch of cayenne pepper and 1 mudra pinch of cumin powder. If you cannot get fresh herbs use dried basil and mint.
- Thinly slice the sweet potato, purple onion, carrots, fennel bulb and courgettes.
- Pour the marinade over the sliced vegetables and let them stand for 62 minutes.
- Place the vegetable slices under the grill and cook for about 11 minutes, turning over as necessary to ensure they cook evenly.
- Spoon the Nut and Seed Da Cream onto a serving dish. Place the grilled vegetables in the middle of the cream, and garnish with fresh basil leaves.
- **For the Nut and Seed Da Cream:** drain the soaked nuts and pumpkin seeds and put into a food processor with 4 cloves of garlic and enough tomato juice to cover all the ingredients. Add 8 drops of tamari and 1 swirl of olive oil. Blend to a smooth, creamy consistency.

Sat Nam

Nut and seed ram cream cheese

You will need
2 handfuls pumpkin seeds
2 handfuls sunflower seeds
2 handfuls mixed nuts
4 garlic cloves
1 handful of fresh mint

From the store cupboard
olive oil
apple cider vinegar
tamari soy sauce
tahini paste
healing water (see p. 25)
toasted sesame seeds (optional)
dried mixed herbs (optional)

This dish was created as an appetiser for a yogic and dairy-free menu, as part of a New Year's Eve celebration dinner in 1999. It is a wonderful accompaniment to any meal, and is also great eaten on its own with bread. Sing, as if welcoming in the New Year with joy in your heart – *God and Me, Me and God are One*.

- Soak the pumpkin and sunflower seeds, and the mixed nuts, in 2 separate bowls for 11 hours.
- Drain the nuts and seeds and place them into a food processor. Add the garlic and fresh mint, 4 swirls of olive oil, 18 drops each of apple cider vinegar and tamari, and 2 generous spoonfuls of tahini paste.
- Blend until a cream cheese consistency is achieved. You may need to add a few drops of healing water to help all the ingredients combine evenly. Taste. Add more tahini if you would like a stronger sesame flavour.
- If serving as an appetiser, mould the mixture into small balls. Roll half the balls in toasted sesame seeds and the other half in dried mixed herbs. Serve with a salad of baby greens or pitta bread.
- Alternatively, use this dish as you would the dairy variety of cream cheese.

Sat Nam

Mediterranean hey vegetable stew

You will need
2 onions, diced
1 leek, sliced
7 garlic cloves, crushed
4 potatoes, peeled and diced
4 carrots, peeled and diced
4 courgettes (zucchini), peeled and diced
4 tomatoes, roughly chopped
1 handful pumpkin seeds
1 handful sesame seeds
1 handful parsley, roughly chopped

From the store cupboard
cumin seeds
paprika
turmeric
healing water (see p. 25)
yogic or organic stock (bouillon) cubes (see p. 27)
tamari soy sauce

A traditional stew is made with meat, but our Middle Eastern-Mediterranean version is made solely with vegetables, nuts and spices. It is full of flavour and is suitable for large parties as it can be prepared beforehand and left to simmer.

Apart from their versatility, stews are great because they embody the Kundalini Yoga concept of *simran*, which is the goal of meditation. It is a continuous, meditative, longingly-creative feeling that bubbles away lovingly in the background, just like a stew.

Simran is also a spiritual name, and we dedicate this dish to all the people who are called by this name, in particular Seva Simran Kaur of London (Eve de Meza), who is a wonderful teacher of Kundalini Yoga.

- Dry-sauté the onions, leek and garlic cloves in a large saucepan over a medium heat. Sprinkle with a few drops of healing water if the mixture starts to caramelise and stick to the pan.
- Add the potatoes, carrots, courgettes and tomatoes. Mix, tracing the outline of a triangle.
- Add 1 mudra pinch each of the cumin seeds, paprika and turmeric.
- Pour in enough healing water to just cover the vegetables. Crumble over 2 stock cubes.
- Add a swirl of tamari, or to taste, and bring to the boil. Simmer uncovered until the liquid has reduced and the vegetables are tender.
- Whilst the stew is cooking, roast the pumpkin and sesame seeds in a frying pan over a low heat. Cool slightly, then mix with the chopped parsley.
- To serve, spoon the vegetable stew into deep bowls and sprinkle over the roasted seed and parsley mix.

Sat Nam

Seaweed, vegetable and avocado salad

You will need
1 packet (50 g/1¾ oz) wakame seaweed
2 avocados, diced
2 cucumbers, diced
2 radishes, sliced
juice of 1 lemon
1 thumb-length nub fresh ginger root, grated
1 garlic clove, crushed

From the store cupboard
olive oil
tamari soy sauce
sesame seeds

This salad can be served either as a main course, as it is rich in proteins and packed with vitamins and minerals, or as part of a meal. It is particularly delicious when served with an assortment of steamed root vegetables.

- Soak the seaweed in warm water until soft. Drain and place in a large salad bowl together with the avocado, cucumber and radish. Mix well whilst chanting *Guru Ram Das*.
- Drizzle the dressing (see below) over the seaweed salad. Sprinkle with sesame seeds and serve.
- **For the dressing:** mix until well combined the juice of 1 lemon, 3 swirls of olive oil, the grated ginger and crushed garlic and 11 drops of tamari.

Sat Nam

Nut, seed and vegetable har bake

You will need
1 handful flax seeds (linseeds)
4 medium potatoes
2 onions, diced
1 leek, sliced
4 large carrots, grated
1 double handful pumpkin seeds
1 double handful sunflower seeds
1 double handful mixed nuts, chopped
mixed fresh herbs (for garnish)

From the store cupboard
healing water (see p. 25)
yogic spice or garam masala (see p. 27)
turmeric
tamari soy sauce
olive oil

This dish has manifold blessings because it tastes heavenly; it permeates the whole house with a warm, delicious aroma; it is very nutritious; and it can be eaten either warm as a complete meal or cold as a snack. Made from root vegetables, it is also a heart-opening bake. For all these reasons, the joyous *Guru Mantra of Ecstasy* (see p. 155) is a wonderful chant to accompany this dish.

When chanting, take up the following position: kneel on your left leg so that your left heel is resting between your left and your right buttock and your right thigh is up against your chest; bring your palms together at the centre of your chest as if in prayer; focus your gaze on the top of your nose and chant for 22 minutes.

- Pre-heat the oven to 180°C/350°F/gas mark 4.
- Place the flax seeds into a food processor with 2 double handfuls of healing water. Soak for 17 minutes before blending.
- Boil the potatoes, onions and leek in a saucepan of healing water. When soft, drain. Remove the skin from the potatoes, then mash them with the onions and leeks.
- Add the 'mash' to the soaked flax seeds in the food processor. Blend until you achieve a thick and sticky consistency. Add 1 mudra pinch each of yogic spice (or garam masala) and turmeric, 18 drops of tamari and 3 swirls of olive oil. Blend again.
- Remove the potato mixture from the food processor and set aside.
- Rinse the food processor's mixing bowl. Add the grated carrots to the clean bowl and purée with 1 swirl of tamari. If too dry, add a little healing water.
- Take a suitably sized, shallow baking tray and spread half the potato mixture over the whole bottom. Sprinkle over half the pumpkin seeds, sunflower seeds and chopped mixed nuts. Next, spread over the carrot purée, followed by the remaining seeds and nuts. Finally, spread over the remaining potato mixture.
- Place in the pre-heated oven and cook for 45–62 minutes, or until the top has turned golden. Remove from the oven and sprinkle with the chopped mixed herbs.
- Serve warm with salad.

Sat Nam

Nut and herb burgers

You will need
1 double handful mixed nuts
1 double handful mixed seeds
1 handful cornflour
1 handful fresh coriander (cilantro)
1 handful fresh parsley
1 thumb-length nub fresh ginger root, finely grated
2 garlic cloves, crushed
2 large potatoes (optional)

From the store cupboard
olive oil
tamari soy sauce
cayenne pepper
sesame seeds
dried mint (optional)
sea salt

Makes approximately 8 burgers

Loaded with seeds and nuts, and therefore protein, these burgers are a nutritious taste sensation that everyone in your family will enjoy. It is also a great dish to make with children, chanting the *Guru Mantra* (see p. 155) as you mix then shape the burgers.

- Mix the nuts, seeds, cornflour, 3 swirls of olive oil and 1 splash of tamari in a food processor.
- Roughly chop the fresh coriander and parsley. Add to the food processor.
- Add the ginger, garlic and 1 small gyan pinch of cayenne pepper. Blend all the ingredients together to form a rough paste, adding water a little at a time if the mixture is too dry. Taste and adjust the flavours, if necessary.
- With wet hands, grab small handfuls of the mixture and shape into small burgers, chanting *Wha-hay Guroo* as you go along.
- Coat each burger with sesame seeds. Heat a frying pan with 1 or 2 swirls of olive oil. When hot, place a couple of burgers into the pan, cooking until heated through and each side has browned. You may need additional oil to cook all the burgers.
- Serve on a bed of salad leaves or with mashed potato (see below).
- **For the mashed potato:** boil the potatoes until tender. Cool slightly, peel and mash in a bowl with 1 mudra pinch of dried mint and 1 splash of olive oil. Season with sea salt.

Sat Nam

Polenta gobinde with red and green creams

You will need
1 double handful polenta
200 ml (7 fl oz/⅘ cup) coconut milk
1 handful mint
1 handful basil
1 garlic clove, crushed
200 ml (7 fl oz/⅘ cup) tomato purée
4 sun-dried tomatoes

From the store cupboard
healing water (see p. 25)
turmeric
yogic or organic stock (bouillon) cube (see p. 27)
olive oil
tamari soy sauce
dried oregano
ground black pepper
sea salt

This is a delicious main course dish that is ideal for special occasions. It is a unique meal, as the corn is very energising, and the creams balance both the lower chakras and the heart centre.

- Fill a large saucepan with healing water. You will require 4 parts water to 1 part polenta.
- Bring the water to the boil and add 1 mudra pinch of turmeric and 1 stock cube, crumbled.
- Lower the heat, then add 1 large swirl of olive oil.
- Slowly pour the polenta into the water (see above). Stir, tracing the outline of the infinity symbol, until the polenta is well combined and begins to free itself from the pan as you stir.
- Remove the saucepan from the heat and divide the cooked polenta between 4 bowls. Cool, then place in the refrigerator to chill.
- When the polenta is cold, turn out of the bowls to form 'discs'. Place under the grill to warm.
- Arrange on a serving platter, then drizzle over the Red and Green Creams (see below).
- **For the Green Cream:** combine the coconut milk with the mint, basil and garlic, mixing well. Season with tamari, to taste.
- **For the Red Cream:** blend the tomato purée with the sun-dried tomatoes, dried oregano and 2 swirls of olive oil. Season with ground black pepper and sea salt, to taste.

Sat Nam

TOP Nut and herb burgers
ABOVE Polenta gobinde with red and green creams

Ha-tha melon in chilli syrup

You will need

- 1 handful raw sugar
- 1 small red chilli, seeded and diced
- 1 thumb-length nub fresh ginger root, grated
- juice of 1 lime
- 1 small cantaloupe (rock melon), diced
- 1 small honeydew melon
- 1 bunch seedless green grapes

Ha means the sun and *Tha* means the moon. Like yin and yang, both should be in balance. This dish is about balancing the coolness of the melon (moon energies) with the fiery nature of the chilli (sun energies), to yield an interesting dish of contrasting tastes.

- Combine the sugar with a little water in a saucepan. Stir over a low heat until the sugar dissolves. Once dissolved, add a little more water and continue to stir until the mixture turns to a syrup.
- Add the chilli and ginger and boil for a maximum of 10 minutes. Strain, then add the lime juice.
- Cut the melons in half, scoop out the seeds and cut into bite-sized chunks. Halve the grapes. Add all the fruit to a glass bowl.
- Pour the syrup over the fruit and toss until well combined. Chill.
- Serve the salad either on its own or with your favourite natural yoghurt (if you're not on the Fruit, Nut and Vegetable Diet).

Sat Nam

Nut and seed energy trifle balls

You will need
17 dates, pitted
healing water (see p. 25)
2 double handfuls nut and seed mix (see p. 94)
1 double handful carob powder
honey
desiccated (shredded) coconut

Makes approximately 22 trifle balls

Children are an important part of the Kundalini Yoga world, since they are the future guardians. Nowhere are children more celebrated than at the annual camps and festivals. They camp outdoors with their parents, attend yoga classes and make new friends. Raising healthy, happy and holy children is part of the Kundalini Yoga *dharma*, path. This dish is a delicious and healthy snack that will re-energise your children in an instant. The main ingredient, the date, is full of the healing properties of the number eight, which relates to heart-centred practices and the planet Saturn.

- Place the dates in a bowl. Cover with just-boiled healing water for a few minutes.
- Drain the dates, reserving the liquid, and place them into a food processor. Pour in half of the reserved liquid. Turn the processor on to a medium speed.
- Slowly pour in the nut and seed mix. Add the carob powder and more of the date water if needed to form a rough paste. Be careful not to add so much liquid that the paste becomes too sticky to roll into smooth balls with your hands. For a sweeter version, add a little honey.
- Remove the paste from the food processor to a glass bowl. Chill in the refrigerator for 62 minutes.
- When chilled, tear off small portions of the trifle mix, each about the size of a walnut, and roll between your hands into balls. Smile and chant your favoured mantra as you do this.
- To finish, roll each ball in desiccated coconut.
- These wonderful morsels can be served immediately or kept covered in the refrigerator for several days.

Sat Nam

Pure harmony nut and seed mix

You will need
1 double handful walnuts
1 double handful Brazil nuts
1 double handful pecans
1 double handful almonds
1 handful macadamia nuts
1 handful hazelnuts
1 handful cashew nuts
1 handful pistachio nuts
1 handful pumpkin seeds
1 handful sunflower seeds
honey

In many of the recipes in this chapter we use mixed nuts, but this is the ultimate mix that can be kept covered with a cotton cloth or tea towel in the refrigerator, or any other cool and dry place. The list of seeds and nuts is extensive, so whatever you can get at the time is fine. Slowly build up your supplies to match our suggested combination. This will ensure you receive optimum benefit from your mix, including a full range of amino acids – the building blocks to the protein that your body needs.

So start your own Pure Harmony Nut and Seed Mix today. Use it in salads, soups, creams or as a nutritious snack. If you are a vegan, also use it in 'milks' and 'cheeses'.

- To obtain the maximum enzyme yield all the nuts and seeds are soaked. Soak the walnuts, Brazil nuts and pecans together in cold water for 11 hours, or overnight.
- In a separate bowl, soak the almonds in cold water for 11 hours, or overnight.
- In a separate bowl soak the macadamia nuts, hazelnuts, cashews and pistachios for 8 hours.
- In a separate bowl, soak the pumpkin and sunflower seeds for 8 hours.
- Drain the almonds and remove the skins. If the skins do not come off easily, soak them again in boiling water for 10 seconds. Drain and peel.
- Drain all the other nuts and seeds and leave them to dry with the almonds on a tray covered with a clean tea towel.
- Mix all of the nuts and seeds in one large bowl and serve as a snack with honey.

Sat Nam

Nut and seed milk

You will need
1 double handful almonds or hazelnuts
healing water (see p. 25)
4 pitted dates or honey

Note: 2 double handfuls of liquid equals 250ml, 8 fl oz or 1 cup.

This is a far tastier version of the shop-bought almond milk. Being homemade, it is much more nutritious, and you can also adjust the overall taste and sweetness to your own liking. You can even try making a milk from a combination of almonds and hazelnuts.

Yogi Bhajan was very specific about not soaking almonds in hot water as the heat drives the tannic acid into the nut. In the event you cannot remove the almond skins from the soaked almonds, we suggest, in this recipe and others, that you soak them in boiling water for an additional 10 seconds.

- Soak the almonds or hazelnuts for 11 hours, or overnight.
- Drain the nuts and place in a food processor. If using almonds, peel off their skins. If the skins do not come off easily, soak them again in boiling water for 10 seconds. Drain and peel.
- Add 6–8 double handfuls of healing water. The less water you use the thicker and creamier the 'milk'. Add 4 pitted dates or a swirl of honey for sweetness. Blend until smooth.
- Serve on its own as a beverage, as part of Yogi Tea, in soups or as a creamy sauce with a fresh fruit salad.

Sat Nam

Vegetable spaghetti with yogic sauce (see p. 96)

Vegetable spaghetti with yogic sauce

You will need
2 butternut squash (pumpkins)
2 carrots
2 courgettes (zucchini)
1 handful fresh mint, roughly chopped
1 handful fresh coriander (cilantro), roughly chopped

From the store cupboard
1 can (400 ml/14 fl oz) coconut milk
yogic spice or garam masala (see p. 27)
cayenne pepper
turmeric
paprika
tamari soy sauce

(pictured on page 95)

The jewel in the crown of Italian cuisine is without any doubt pasta. When Italians emigrated, settling throughout the New World and Oceania, they brought their pasta with them. From there, pasta found its way into everyone's lifestyle. It is a worldwide comfort food – traditional pasta, made from wheat, is both fulfilling and satisfying. The spaghetti in this dish – made from fresh, raw vegetables – is equally so. With no processed flours, salts or sugars it is, however, a much more energy-rich option. Eaten raw with Yogic Sauce, it is a great 'living' dish, full of vitamins and enzymes. Enjoy the *prana*!

- Cut the butternut squash, carrots and courgettes into long and fine, matchstick-thin strips. Alternatively, you may have access to a mandolin, which means it will take less time to prepare this dish, and you will get very even and fine julienne strips.
- Toss the prepared vegetables together and place a handful or two on each dinner plate.
- To serve, spoon over the Yogic Sauce (see below) and garnish with chopped fresh mint and coriander.
- **For the Yogic Sauce:** bring the coconut milk to the boil in a medium-sized pan. Add 1 mudra pinch each of the yogic spice (or garam masala), cayenne pepper, turmeric and paprika. Reduce the heat to low. Add a swirl of tamari, then simmer until the liquid reduces by half.

Sat Nam

Fasting

Fasting forms part of the Kundalini Yoga tradition, though not all practitioners undertake this path. Physically, fasting gives your body time to rest, and mentally, it is a time to build strength of mind. Do ensure, however, that you consult your physician before undertaking any fast. Also, fasting is not recommended for women who are pregnant or lactating, and children. Here we include a few basic guidelines to fasting and three different fruit fasts.

Prepare yourself for fasting by adjusting your general diet beforehand. To do this, stop eating junk food and make your meals light and healthy by including more fresh fruit, vegetables, grains and pulses. Also, try to skip one or two meals each day. For example don't eat breakfast and enjoy lunch as your first meal.

- Don't fast too often as this will make your system weak.
- Traditionally, people avoid company when fasting – utilise this time in *sadhana* (yogic spiritual practice).
- Whilst fasting, don't dream or pine for food. By constantly thinking of food, you will inhibit your ability to achieve your desired results.
- Don't make a fuss about your fast. The observance of such a *niyama*, or negative state of mind, is positive for your spiritual advancement, but dwelling is not.
- Only drink healing water (see p. 25), spring, mineral and filtered water and Yogi Tea (see p. 26).
- Don't eat heavy foods or use seasonings when breaking (concluding) a fast. Drink milk or fruit juice, and avoid coffee and alcohol.

THE FRUIT FAST

It is good to do the Fruit Fast in the spring, as this is a time of new beginnings. A general Fruit Fast is completed over 30 days. Eat one type of fruit at a time and be sensible about how much – don't over-eat – three bowls of fruit per day should suffice. If you want, add a small amount of organic yoghurt to your fruit. Don't drink fruit (or vegetable) juice as it is highly concentrated. Below are two examples of recipes you can make when on a Fruit Fast.

Mango Salad

Cut 1 mango into small cubes. Place the cubes in a glass bowl and squeeze over the juice of half a lemon. Chop up a few leaves of fresh mint and sprinkle them on the top. Mix with love.

Avocado Salad

Avocado is a fine fruit that can be used as a variation to other, sweeter fruits. Cut 1 large or 2 small avocados, into cubes. Mix the cubes with the juice of 1 lemon or lime, then sprinkle on a few drops of tamari soy sauce (optional). You can also add a sprinkling of chopped fresh basil leaves.

THE MELON FAST

The Melon Fast is a great diet to follow if you want to cleanse the liver, intestines and kidneys. Cantaloupe (rock melon) is both warming and a good natural laxative, watermelon is cooling and is very good for both the liver and the kidneys, and papaya (pawpaw) aids digestion. The Melon Fast is, however, a very dynamic diet and should only be followed by people who are experienced in fasting.

The recommended time to start this fast is summer when the weather is hot. It is also recommended that you massage your body daily with almond oil.

The duration of the Melon Fast is either 21 or 27 days. On the first day of breaking the fast, eat a different type of fruit at each meal. On the second day, again eat a different type of fruit at each meal, but add yoghurt to the fruit. On the third day, start to include soups and steamed vegetables at each meal.

Days 1–3: cantaloupe (rock melon)
Days 4–6: watermelon
Days 7–9: papaya (pawpaw)
Days 10–12: drink hot healing water with lemon and honey only
Days 13–15: drink warm healing water only
Days 16–18: drink hot healing water with lemon and honey only
Days 19–21: papaya
Days 22–24: watermelon
Days 25–27: cantaloupe

To complete the Melon Fast over 21 days rather than 28 days, cut back days 10–12, 13–15 and 16–18 from 3 days to 1.

BANANA FAST

This is a mono-diet and should only be undertaken by those who are experienced in fasting. The Banana Fast is very good for detoxification, removing drug deposits from the medulla in the brain and rebuilding worn body tissue. Start this diet in the spring on a new moon, and continue it for 15 days. Drink a minimum of 8 glasses of healing water each day. You can also drink Yogi Tea. No dairy is allowed except for a small amount of milk in the Yogi Tea.

1 hour before breakfast: 1 glass fresh orange juice, sweetened with honey.
Breakfast: 3 bananas, including their stringy fibres. Eat these very slowly, juicing each bite in your mouth. Once you finish eating the bananas, finish the meal by chewing on the seeds of 1 cardamom pod. This will help with the digestion of the bananas.
Lunch and dinner: same as for breakfast, excluding the orange juice.
After the 15th day: drink warm water with honey and lemon for 1 day, then do the Mung Beans and Rice Diet for 28 days (see Chapter 5). During this period you also eat fruit between meals and drink Yogi Tea.

Sat Nam

Yogic vegetables with rainbow party sauces (see pp. 112–13)

7 Food to share

Barbecue to dinner party food

The sharing of food forms a very important part of the Kundalini Yoga path, where there is an emphasis on community service and helping the needy. This approach originates from Sikhism and the communal kitchen or *langar*. The food is free and everyone is welcome, regardless of religion, gender, creed or social status. In every *gurdwara* (Sikh place of worship) there is a *langar*. Everyone helps prepare the meals that are then eaten sitting on the floor.

The *langar* started 500 years ago, when there were no charitable institutions to cater for the poor and the travellers. Guru Nanak founded the village Kartarpur, Lahore, where he settled and started farming. From the fruits of his work, he started a charitable social service providing food for the needy. Guru Nanak advised his disciples to do the same, and the successive Sikh Gurus continued with this practice; a tradition that later became known as Guru's *langar*.

Indeed, the inspiration for this chapter came from the many wonderful meals we have shared with friends, family and fellow yogis during our yogic journey. It is about using food to nurture, honouring Kundalini Yoga's rich heritage of sharing and serving the community. Since Kundalini Yoga food is prepared and served with love, it tastes so much better when shared with loved ones. There is no need for expensive ingredients, complicated recipes and luxurious settings to enjoy a good meal.

Chapatti

You will need
12 double handfuls wholewheat flour, sifted
sea salt
warm healing water (see p. 125)
oil
oil or ghee (optional)

Note: 2 double handfuls liquid equals 250 ml, 8 fl oz or 1 cup

Makes 31 pieces

Chapatti, or skillet bread, is the ubiquitous staple for many an Indian meal. Nothing beats a warm, freshly made chapatti, torn into pieces with your fingers and dipped into a rich gravy or curry. The texture of the bread absorbs all the flavours, so that your tastebuds are treated to the full glory of the dish. Although chapattis can be bought in packets, freshly made ones are so much better. Once you have made your first batch, never again will you settle for anything less.

While you are making the chapatti try chanting the *Adi Shakti*. This first *Shakti* mantra tunes into the frequency of the Divine Mother and to the primal, protective and generating energies. Chanting it eliminates fears and fulfils desires (see p. 155).

- With your hands, mix together the flour and salt in a large bowl.
- Make a well in the centre of the mixture, then slowly add the healing water in stages and massage the dough. Keep adding water and massaging the dough until it pulls cleanly away from the sides of the bowl. The firmer the dough the easier it will be to roll; however a softer dough will result in softer chapattis.
- Lightly oil a clean work surface and knead the dough for 11–15 minutes.
- Return the mixture to a lightly oiled glass bowl. Cover with a damp tea towel and let the dough rest for approximately 2 hours.
- When the dough is ready, flour your hands and the work surface. Divide the dough into 31 pieces. Roll each piece into a ball, then flatten into rounds. Keep the dough pieces and rounds under a damp tea towel so they don't dry out whilst you are cooking.
- Heat a skillet or heavy frying pan and throw the chapatti rounds in one or two at a time. Fry until they puff up, then flip over and cook until the other side also puffs up.
- Brush each chapatti with oil or ghee, if you like, then remove it from the heat and keep covered with a cloth in a dish in a warm oven until the rest are cooked.
- Chapatti-making is traditionally a social activity, so invite your friends over to share the task of kneading, rolling, flattening and cooking – and don't forget to chant the mantra *Adi Shakti*.

Sat Nam

Aura-white tofu with coconut and quinoa

You will need
4 garlic cloves, crushed
1 thumb-length nub fresh ginger root, grated
1 stick lemon grass
4–5 lime leaves
1 small red chilli, seeded and thinly sliced
1 purple onion, chopped
4 carrots, diced
1 broccoli head, cut into florets
1 red (sweet) pepper, seeded and diced
1 yellow (sweet) pepper, seeded and diced
7 white mushrooms, sliced
1 small block (180 g/ 6⅓ oz) firm tofu
1 block (150 g/5 oz) creamed coconut
4 handfuls quinoa

Store cupboard ingredients
coriander seeds
healing water (see p.25)
yogic or organic stock (bouillon) cubes (see p. 27)
1 bay leaf
turmeric
garam masala
tamari soy sauce
tahini paste

This is a high-protein, chakra-energy enhancing, celebratory dish, and a fully balanced meal in itself. The quinoa is the mother of all grains, and has been part of human diet for 5000 years. Originally one of the three staple foods of the Incas, along with corn and potatoes, quinoa is very high in protein and is widely available today.

Serve this protein-rich dish with a Baby Green and Sesame Salad (see below), and enjoy this heart-opening and aura-enhancer dish with your family and friends.

- Dry-fry the garlic with 2 mudra pinches of coriander seeds in a large saucepan.
- Fill the saucepan with healing water until three-quarters full. Add 1 crushed stock cube. Bring the water to the boil.
- Add the ginger, lemon grass, lime leaves and sliced red chilli. Combine well.
- Next, add the prepared vegetables and 1 bay leaf.
- Cut the tofu blocks into cubes and grate the creamed coconut. Add both to the vegetable mix. Sprinkle over 2 mudra pinches each of the turmeric and garam marsala, and 18 drops of tamari. Combine.
- Bring the mixture to the boil then add the quinoa. Lower the heat, cover and cook for 22 minutes, or until the quinoa has opened up. Serve with a Baby Green and Sesame Salad (see p. 43).

Sat Nam

Magadra siri rice and green lentils

You will need
1 handful white basmati rice
1 double handful green lentils
3 garlic cloves, finely chopped
1 small handful fresh parsley, chopped
½ small onion, diced (optional)

From the store cupboard
ground cumin
cayenne pepper
paprika
turmeric
yogic or organic stock (bouillon) cube (see p. 27)
healing water (see p. 25)
olive oil
ghee

This is a traditional North African dish, which is very healthy as it combines rice with green lentils, resulting in a balanced protein and carbohydrate meal.

Whilst the rice and lentils are cooking, take the time to learn the words of the mantra *Ajai Alai* (see p. 155). This is from the *Jaap Sahib* – a great, poetic offering to the One Almighty Wahe Guru, composed by the tenth Sikh Master Guru Gobind Singh. It brings greater sensitivity to the Being, and nurtures the ability to intuitively understand what people say.

- Place the rice and green lentils into a large saucepan. Dry-fry with the garlic for 2 minutes, adding a few drops of water, if required, to stop burning.
- Add 1 mudra pinch of cumin and a small gyan pinch cayenne pepper, paprika and turmeric. Combine, tracing the outline of the infinity symbol as you stir.
- Add 1 stock cube and enough healing water to double the level of the rice and lentils.
- Bring to the boil and simmer until the rice and lentils are tender. This will take approximately 15 minutes. Add 1 swirl of olive oil and sprinkle with the chopped fresh parsley.
- For additional flavour, you can also sprinkle over the rice and lentils half a diced onion that has been fried with 1 swirl of olive oil, or 1 spoonful ghee, until golden (optional).
- Serve with yoghurt on the side and a tomato and cucumber salad.

Sat Nam

Baked filo guru roll

You will need
6 generous double handfuls baby spinach
4 garlic cloves, finely chopped
1 large block (450 g/1 lb) feta, cubed
3 spoonfuls ghee
3 sheets filo pastry
1 large block (450g/1 lb) fresh tofu, cubed (variation)

From the store cupboard
olive oil
sea salt
dried mint
sesame seeds

This is a simple and fulfilling yogic dish from Turkey. Traditionally made with feta cheese, it is equally delicious when made with tofu, simply replace the feta with fresh tofu. Whilst baking this dish, call upon Guru Ram Das in praise of his spiritual guiding light and protective grace, by chanting *Guroo Guroo Wha-hay Guroo, Guroo Raam Daas Guroo*.

- Heat the oven to 180°C/350°F/gas mark 4.
- Add the baby spinach and garlic to a heated frying pan. Mix well then combine with 2 swirls of olive oil, 1 pinch of dried mint and sea salt, to taste. Take off the heat once the spinach has wilted, toss through the feta (or tofu), and cool.
- Oil your hands and the work surface with olive oil.
- Place 1 sheet of filo pastry on the work surface so that the longer edge is parallel to you.
- Brush its entire surface lightly with ghee (or olive oil). Repeat with two more sheets of pastry, placing the sheets on top of each other.
- Spread the spinach filling along the longer edge of the filo pastry. Roll up tightly, tucking in the sides of the filo as you do. Brush with more ghee and sprinkle with sesame seeds.
- Bake in the pre-heated oven for 15 minutes or until golden and the pastry is crisp.
- Serve with salad and Sesame Sauce (see p. 75).

Sat Nam

TOP Magadra siri rice and green lentils
ABOVE Baked filo guru rolls

Tofu with red and green sauces

You will need
1 block (180 g/6⅓ oz) soft silken tofu
2 garlic cloves, crushed
1 handful fresh basil leaves
1 handful fresh parsley
1 large tomato, diced
1 red (sweet) pepper, diced

From the store cupboard
1 handful rice flour
1 handful desiccated (shredded) coconut
olive oil
sea salt
white pepper
balsamic vinegar

One of the most healing and effective ingredients in the food you cook is the 'vibration' you put into it whilst cooking. By chanting as you cook, the power of the mantra has the ability to nourish, sustain, and energise the body. This dish comes with the colour vibration of the root chakra, associated with the colour red, and heart chakra, associated with the colour green. As you prepare this dish vibrate the sound *Om Om Om*, and feel the Infinite rise from the root chakra to the heart chakra and then into the dish.

- Heat your oven to 180°C/350°F/gas mark 4.
- Place the tofu into a food processor and blend to a smooth paste.
- Add the rice flour, desiccated coconut, 1 garlic clove, 3 swirls of olive oil and 1 small gyan pinch each of sea salt and white pepper. Whiz until combined. If you are watching your weight, leave out the desiccated coconut as it is high in calories.
- Mould the mixture into 4–6 balls. Add more rice flour if it is too sticky.
- Place the balls on an oiled baking sheet, flatten slightly, and bake for 10–15 minutes.
- Remove the balls from the oven and arrange on a serving dish with the Green and Red Sauces (see below).
- **For the Green Sauce:** place the basil, parsley, 1 small pinch of sea salt and 1 swirl of olive oil into a food processor. Blend until smooth. Adjust seasoning, to taste.
- **For the Red Sauce:** place the tomato, red pepper, 1 garlic clove, 1 swirl of olive oil, 1 swirl of balsamic vinegar and 1 small pinch of sea salt into a food processor. Blend until smooth. Adjust seasoning, to taste.

Sat Nam

Ashram beans

You will need
4 handfuls adzuki beans
3 garlic cloves, finely chopped
1 thumb-length nub fresh ginger root, finely grated
2 medium onions, diced

From the store cupboard
healing water (see p. 25)
sea salt
coriander seeds
cumin seeds
chilli flakes
ghee (or butter)

One of the main criteria of *ashram* food is that it's cheap to make; another is that it tastes good. Beans are cheap, nutritious and absorb flavours beautifully, so that each mouthful you take is redolent of the spices used in the dish.

- Soak the adzuki beans overnight in plenty of water.
- Drain the beans and place in a large saucepan. Add the garlic and ginger. Cover with healing water, bring to the boil and simmer for 1 hour before adding 1 mudra pinch of sea salt. Boil for a further 20–30 minutes, or until cooked.
- In a heated frying pan, dry-fry the onions with 1 mudra pinch each of coriander seeds, cumin seeds and chilli flakes (if you like your food spicy, add more chilli). The onions and spices can also be fried in a lightly oiled skillet using either ghee or butter.
- Take the cooked beans off the heat and drain. Reserve the water.
- Mash the cooked beans as you would boiled potatoes, adding the reserved water, spoonful by spoonful, until you get a creamy consistency. Add some ghee, to taste.
- Spoon in the fried onions and spices and mix thoroughly. Serve hot.

Sat Nam

Yogi hummus

You will need
2 double handfuls chickpeas
1 double handful tahini paste
juice of 1 lemon
3 garlic cloves, chopped
parsley leaves (for garnish)

Store cupboard ingredients
ground cumin
sea salt
olive oil

Note: 2 double handfuls liquid equals 250 ml, 8 fl oz or 1 cup

(pictured on page 107)

What makes hummus special is that it is often eaten as a finger-food with bread. In Kundalini Yoga, the hand is a very important part of the body as it is where the *nadis*, or energy channels, end. By holding your fingers in specific positions, the energy flow is guided through the body, stimulating the brain. There are many different finger positions, known as mudras, used when practising yoga. When used, your fingers are talking to the different parts of your mind and body.

- Soak the chickpeas overnight: 2 parts water to 1 part chickpeas.
- Drain the soaked chickpeas, then place in a saucepan and cover with water. Bring to the boil and simmer until tender. This will take 1–2 hours.
- Once cooked, drain the chickpeas. Place into a food processor and blend.
- Add the tahini paste, lemon juice, chopped garlic, 1 large pinch of ground cumin, 1 small gyan pinch of sea salt and 2 generous swirls of olive oil. Blend until you achieve a smooth paste. Adjust seasoning, to taste.
- Garnish with a sprinkling of ground cumin and several parsley leaves.

Sat Nam

Red, orange and green falafel

You will need
2 double handfuls chickpeas
4 garlic cloves, crushed
1 handful fresh parsley, chopped
1 sweet potato (yam), peeled, boiled and puréed
1 red (sweet) pepper, de-seeded and finely chopped

From the store cupboard
baking powder
olive oil
ground coriander
ground cumin
paprika (pimento)

Chakras are individual spinning wheels of energy that are found in the human body at precise locations. Each has a particular effect on a person's mind and body.

The root chakra is red, the colour of passion and general physical wellbeing; the sacral chakra is orange, the colour of health and vitality; and the heart chakra is green, the colour of warmth and love. This colourful dish represents these three colours. Share it with your friends and feel well, happy and loved.

While you are blending the falafel mixture you can chant *Saa Taa Naa Maa*. This is the *Panj Shabad* mantra expressing the five primal sounds of the universe. 'S' is infinity, 'T' is life, 'N' is death and 'M' is rebirth. The fifth sound, 'A', connects the other letters to give one of the most frequently used mantras in Kundalini Yoga.

- Soak the chickpeas in a glass bowl overnight: 2 parts water to 1 part chickpeas.
- Heat the oven to 200°C/400°F/gas mark 6.
- Crush the chickpeas and garlic together with the baking powder and a few drops of olive oil until you achieve a rough paste that feels moist. Alternatively, mix the ingredients in a food processor. If the mixture is dry, add a few extra drops of oil.
- Divide the mixture into three portions. Each portion will be used to make 1 of 3 different versions of falafel. Whilst doing this chant *Saa Taa Naa Maa*.
- For the green portion, add the chopped parsley and I mudra pinch of ground coriander. Mix well.
- For the orange portion, add the puréed sweet potato and 1 mudra pinch of ground cumin. Mix well.
- For the red portion, add the chopped red pepper plus 1 mudra pinch of paprika. Mix well.
- Roll each mixture into small balls about the size of a walnut. You will get about 6 balls per mixture.
- Place the falafel on a lightly oiled baking sheet and place in the pre-heated oven.
- Bake until the falafel turns a lovely, even golden brown. This will take between 22 and 31 minutes.
- Serve with a variety of salads, Yogi Hummus (see p. 105), Sesame and Mint Sauce (see p. 108) and pitta bread.

Sat Nam

TOP Green falafel
CENTRE RIGHT Yellow falafel
CENTRE LEFT Yogi hummus (see p. 105)
BOTTOM Red falafel

Yogi's tofu skewers with sesame mint sauce

You will need
1 block (450 g/1 lb) tofu
juice of 2 lemons
3 garlic cloves, finely chopped
1 small onion, finely chopped
1 thumb-length nub fresh ginger root, finely grated
juice of 1 orange
1 handful fresh mint, chopped
1 handful fresh coriander (cilantro), chopped
1 double handful Sesame and Mint Sauce (see below)

From the store cupboard
olive oil
tamari soy sauce
tahini paste
sea salt
bamboo skewers

Note: 2 double handfuls liquid equals 250 ml, 8 fl oz or 1 cup

Barbecued food, shared with friends outdoors, is delicious. But what do you do at a vegetarian or vegan barbecue? Yogi's Tofu Skewers with Sesame Mint Sauce. To make the whole event stress free, you can either prepare the skewers beforehand or even prepare and freeze them. They are, however, best made fresh as they keep their full flavour and appearance.

If your friends are travelling home after your barbecue, chant the *Mangala Charn* mantra, to surround the human-magnetic field with protective light (see p. 155).

- Slice the tofu into medium-sized cubes (approximately 20 cubes).
- Place in a glass bowl and pour over the juice of 1 lemon, garlic, onion, grated ginger, 4 swirls of olive oil and 1 swirl of tamari. Marinate for a minimum of 62 minutes.
- Prepare the Sesame and Mint Sauce (see below) whilst the tofu is marinating.
- Slide 5 pieces of the tofu on to each bamboo skewer. (Pre-soak the skewers in water to help stop the wood burning during cooking.)
- Place the skewers on to the barbecue charcoals or under a grill on a medium setting. Cook until golden brown on all sides. This will take 3–4 minutes.
- Drizzle the sauce over the hot tofu skewers and serve.
- **For the Sesame and Mint Sauce:** mix 2 double handfuls tahini paste with the juice of 1 lemon, the orange juice, mint, coriander and 1 pinch of sea salt. Stir tracing the outline of the infinity symbol until you get a well-combined and smooth consistency.

Sat Nam

Heart-opening millet and soya bean stew

You will need
- 2 double handfuls soya beans
- 1 thumb-nail square of kombu seaweed
- 2 onions, finely chopped
- 5 garlic cloves, chopped
- 2 single handfuls millet
- 3 tomatoes, diced
- 1 generous handful green beans, topped, tailed and sliced
- 1 handful fresh basil, chopped

From the store cupboard
- cumin seeds
- turmeric
- paprika
- cayenne pepper
- yogic or organic stock (bouillon) cubes (see p. 27)
- healing water (see p. 25)
- sea salt

In the yogic tradition, we tend to use mainly rice in our cooking. It is the most popular grain eaten in Asia, cheap, easy to cook and stores well. In this dish, we substitute rice with millet and soya beans to create a well-balanced meal. It also gives an imaginative dimension to the dish. The millet is cooked rapidly to preserve its nutty flavour.

- Soak the soya beans overnight in water. Change the water a couple of times and ensure the beans are covered by water at all times.
- Drain the beans and simmer until cooked in a large saucepan with plenty of water until soft. This will take approximately 2 hours.
- Add the kombu seaweed – this will help improve digestion of the soya beans. Set aside.
- Place the prepared onions, garlic and millet in another large saucepan. Combine.
- Add 1 mudra pinch each of cumin seeds, turmeric and paprika, and 1 small gyan pinch of cayenne pepper.
- Drain the beans and add to the onion mix along with 2–3 crushed stock cubes, the tomatoes, green beans and fresh basil.
- Stir 3 times. Add healing water to twice the mixture's volume.
- Bring to the boil and boil rapidly until the liquid is completely absorbed by the millet and beans.
- Season with sea salt and serve with a salad of green salad leaves and fresh herbs.

Sat Nam

Bulgur pavan salad

You will need
2 double handfuls bulgur (cracked wheat)
1 large tomato
1 medium red onion
1 orange (sweet) pepper
2 garlic cloves
juice of 1 lemon
1 small bunch fresh parsley, roughly chopped
1 double handful couscous (variation)
2 double handfuls quinoa (variation)

From the store cupboard
healing water (see p. 25)
olive oil
sea salt
black pitted olives

Note: 2 double handfuls liquid equals 250 ml, 8 fl oz or 1 cup

This is a great salad for crowds as it is quick and easy to make. Also, after eating this dish your guests are bound to be very happy and satisfied, since bulgur is full of *prana* – the life force of the Universe that exists within our physical bodies and all around us.

Bulgur, or cracked wheat, only needs a very short cooking time, which involves soaking it in just-boiled water – use this time to chant the *Guru Mantra of Ecstasy* (see p. 155).

As a variation on this dish, for a gluten free meal, replace the bulgur with quinoa. For a dish that is super-quick to make, use couscous.

- Place the bulgur into a glass bowl and pour over 3 double handfuls of boiled healing water.
- Add 1 swirl of olive oil and a sprinkling of sea salt. Cover for 21 minutes and chant *Wha-hay Guroo* whilst you prepare the rest of the ingredients.
- Dice the tomato, red onion, orange pepper and finely chop the garlic. Mix everything together, tracing the outline of the infinity symbol as you stir.
- Squeeze the lemon juice over the vegetables. Add the chopped parsley and 7 finely diced black pitted olives.
- Add the puffed bulgur along with 1 swirl of olive oil. Mix with your hands to bring pranic energy into the salad. Season with sea salt.
- **For the couscous variation:** the ratio is 1 handful of couscous to 250 ml (8 fl oz/1 cup) boiling water. Add the boiling water to the couscous and wait for 5 minutes.
- **For the quinoa variation:** use the same proportion of boiling water to quinoa and cook for 11–15 minutes or until the quinoa has opened up.

Sat Nam

Seven vegetable curry

You will need
3 garlic cloves, crushed
2 medium carrots, peeled and diced
2 medium potatoes, peeled and diced
2 medium beetroots (beet), peeled and diced
1 generous handful green beans, topped, tailed and sliced
2 handfuls frozen peas (or fresh, if available)
2 handfuls corn kernels
2 large tomatoes, chopped
fresh green chilli, to taste

From the store cupboard
olive oil or ghee
turmeric
sea salt
healing water (see p. 25)
yogic or organic stock (bouillon) cubes (see p.27)
curry powder

Seven is a very powerful number – it represents the seven days of creation and the seven planets. It is also the number of the crown chakra. In this dish, however, the use of seven vegetables is as a celebration of bountiful harvest. As a powerful celebratory dish, eat it with blessings and love in your heart. In this recipe we suggest seven vegetables; however, any combination of seven vegetables is fine. Any herbs and salad leaves you use are additional.

- Brush a heavy saucepan with oil or ghee, then heat over a medium setting.
- Add the crushed garlic and brown.
- Add 2 mudra pinches turmeric and dry-fry until you can smell the aroma of the spice.
- Add all the vegetables, except the chilli, and 1 small gyan pinch of sea salt. Cover and cook on a low setting for 3 minutes, stirring only once.
- Add 4 double handfuls of healing water and 4 stock cubes.
- Season with 1 mudra pinch of curry powder. Add sliced fresh chilli, to taste.
- Cook for a further 11 minutes or until the potatoes are cooked.
- Season with sea salt and serve with your favourite type of steamed rice.

Sat Nam

Yogic vegetables with rainbow party sauces

For the grilled vegetables
2 red onions
4 courgettes (zucchini)
1 sweet potato (yam)
2 small aubergines (eggplants)
8 white mushrooms

From the store cupboard
sea salt
olive oil
balsamic vinegar
dried basil
dried mint
cayenne pepper
white pepper
mustard powder
pinch turmeric
tamari soy sauce

For the orange sauce
3 carrots
1 sweet potato (yam)
1 orange (sweet) pepper

For the red sauce
1 red onion
5 tomatoes
1 red (sweet) pepper
1 small cooked beetroot (beet)
1 small red chilli

(pictured on page 98)

This is a fun, colourful and very healthy dish to be enjoyed with your family and friends. Not only do you have the brilliance of the vegetables but also five differently coloured sauces – orange, red, yellow, green and purple – for your guests to dip the lightly cooked vegetables into. Serve everything together for a celebration meal and chakra joy.

For the Grilled Vegetables

- Slice the onions, courgettes, sweet potato and aubergine and place in a large, flat glass dish. Add the mushrooms and sprinkle generously with sea salt. Set aside for 2 hours.
- Wash off the salt and wipe all the vegetables dry with kitchen paper (paper towel).
- Rinse the glass bowl then return the vegetables to it.
- Add 3 swirls of olive oil, 1 swirl of balsamic vinegar, 1 mudra pinch of dried basil and 1 mudra pinch of dried mint.
- Marinate for 62 minutes whilst you make the sauces.
- To cook the vegetables, place them on a barbecue or under a grill on a medium heat.
- Cook for 11 minutes. Turn occasionally to ensure the pieces cook evenly.

For the Orange Sauce

- Thickly slice the carrots, peel and dice the sweet potato, and quarter, de-seed and dice the orange pepper.
- Place all the vegetables into a bamboo steamer over a saucepan of simmering water. Steam until soft.
- Remove the vegetables to a food processor. Add 1 mudra pinch of cayenne pepper and blend until smooth. Season with sea salt.

For the Red Sauce

- Pre-heat your oven to 200°C/400°/gas mark 6F.
- Roughly dice the onion, quarter the tomatoes, quarter and de-seed the red pepper, dice the beetroot and thinly slice the red chilli.
- Place all the vegetables onto an oven-proofed tray. Cover with kitchen foil (aluminum foil).
- Cook for 11 minutes, then remove the vegetables to a food processor.
- Add 2 swirls of olive oil and 1 swirl of balsamic vinegar. Blend until smooth.
- Season with sea salt, to taste.

For the yellow sauce
3 garlic cloves
1 yellow (sweet) pepper
1 thumb-length nub fresh ginger root
2 double handfuls corn kernels, canned, frozen or fresh
juice of 2 lemons

For the green sauce
2 handfuls fresh basil
2 handfuls fresh parsley
2 handfuls fresh mint
2 handfuls fresh rocket (argula)
1 small green chilli
juice of 1 lemon

For the purple sauce
1 small purple cabbage
1 cooked beetroot (beet)
1 handful blueberries
1 purple onion
1 thumb-length nub fresh ginger root
3 garlic cloves

For the Yellow Sauce

- Finely chop the garlic, quarter and de-seed the yellow pepper and grate the ginger.
- Add 1 circular swirl of olive oil to a frying pan. Once the oil is hot, drop in all the prepared fresh yellow vegetables and the corn kernels. Sauté for 3–5 minutes or until the vegetables are al dente.
- Add 1 small gyan pinch of white pepper and 1 mudra pinch each of mustard powder and turmeric.
- Stir 8 times then remove the mixture to a food processor. Blend until you get a semi-smooth consistency.
- Add 2 swirls of olive oil and the juice of 2 lemons. Whiz a few times.
- Season with sea salt, to taste.

For the Green Sauce

- Place the basil, parsley, mint and rocket into a food processor
- Halve, de-seed and roughly chop the green chilli. Add to the mixed herbs.
- Pour over 4 swirls of olive oil, 4 swirls of balsamic vinegar and the juice of 1 lemon.
- Blend until smooth, then season with sea salt, to taste.

For the Purple Sauce

- Slice the cabbage, peel and dice the cooked beetroot, dice the onion, grate the ginger and crush the garlic.
- Place the prepared vegetables into a saucepan over a medium heat. Add the blueberries.
- Sauté with a few drops of water for 3 minutes or until softened. Add additional drops of water if required to avoid burning.
- Place the mix into a food processor with 4 swirls of olive oil, 4 swirls of balsamic vinegar and 1 swirl of tamari.
- Blend until smooth. Season with sea salt, to taste.

Sat Nam

We-are-all-one-party wrap

You will need

For the Indian Wrap

2 handfuls quinoa
1 sweet potato, peeled and diced
1 block (180 g/6⅓ oz) tofu, cubed
1 thumb-length nub fresh ginger root, grated
4 Indian flat bread
Red Sauce (see p. 112)
Green Sauce (see p. 113)

For the Middle Eastern wrap

2 handfuls tahini paste
juice of 1 lemon
1 garlic clove, finely chopped
1 medium tomato, finely diced
1 small bunch fresh parsley, chopped
12–16 Red, Orange and Green Falafel (see p. 106)
4 small wholemeal pitta breads

For the Mexican wrap

2 double handfuls adzuki beans, soaked overnight
1 red chilli, de-seeded and sliced
1 green chilli, de-seeded and sliced
1 small square of kombu seaweed
fresh coriander (cilantro), chopped
2 large tortillas
Vand Chakna Guacomole (see p. 31)
Orange Sauce (optional), (see p. 112)

From the store cupboard

cayenne pepper
olive oil
tamari soy sauce
mustard seeds
healing water (see p. 25)
sea salt

Wraps are one of those great foods that you eat with your fingers; and eating food with your fingers is a wonderful and powerful way to share food with your friends. Food at *langar* (communal kitchen) at every *gurdwara* (Sikh place of worship) is vegetarian and is eaten with your hands whilst sitting on the floor.

The Guru-ka-langar in India was maintained by Guru Arjan and Guru Hargobind. During Guru Hargobind's lifetime (1595–1644), his son, Atal, was in charge. Atal supplied food to the Sikhs in the battlefield, and his service and devotion led to the proverb, *Baba Atal, Pakki Pakai Ghal* ('Baba Atal supply cooked meals'). The three wraps here are our version of *langar* food. They are also great to take on picnics.

Indian Wrap

- Place in a pot the quinoa, sweet potato, tofu and ginger along with 1 small gyan pinch of cayenne pepper, 2 generous swirls of olive oil, 1 small swirl of tamari and 1 mudra pinch of mustard seeds. Combine well, tossing the ingredients with your hands for added energy.
- Add enough healing water to double the level in the pot. Bring to the boil and simmer for 10–15 minutes or until the quinoa has puffed open.
- Cover and let the mixture cool for a short time.
- Fill the Indian flat bread with the quinoa mix. Add the Red and Green Sauces, to taste.

Middle Eastern Wrap

- Mix the tahini paste with the lemon juice and enough healing water to achieve a thick, spreadable consistency.
- Add the crushed garlic and season with sea salt, to taste.
- Spread each pitta bread with the tahini mixture.
- Add 3 or 4 falafel (see p. 106) to each. Sprinkle with diced tomato and chopped parsley.

Mexican Wrap

- Soak the adzuki beans overnight in plenty of water.
- Drain the beans and transfer to a saucepan with the prepared chillies and kombu seaweed.
- Pour in enough healing water to double the level in the pot.
- Bring to the boil and simmer for approximately 1 hour, or until the beans are soft. Drain.
- Add 2 swirls of olive oil and lightly crush with a fork. Add sea salt, to taste.
- Spread the tortillas with the Vand Chakna Guacamole. Pile on the crushed adzuki beans and garnish with fresh coriander. Top with a few spoonfuls of Orange Sauce (see p. 112) (optional). Cut in half and serve.

Sat Nam

TOP Middle Eastern wrap
CENTRE Indian wrap
LEFT Mexican wrap

Yogic apple crumble pie

You will need
4 apples, peeled and grated
1 handful raw sugar
4 handfuls organic rolled oats
1 handful milk
1 handful melted ghee
1 handful desiccated coconut (shredded)
1 handful mixed crushed nuts

Note: 2 double handfuls liquid equals 250 ml, 8 fl oz or 1 cup

Here we have combined the American 'apple pie' with the famous English 'apple crumble'. It is a very healthy cake and a great treat, not only for special occasions but also for every day.

- Heat the oven to 180°C/350°F/gas mark 4.
- Line the bottom of a round 20-cm (8-in) cake tin with a sheet of oiled baking paper.
- Put all the ingredients in a large glass bowl and mix until combined.
- Spoon the apple mix into the prepared cake tin.
- Place in the pre-heated oven and bake for 31 minutes or until the top is golden brown and firm to the touch.
- Remove from the oven. Cool in the tin before serving.

Sat Nam

Corn, mango and banana cake

You will need
2 double handfuls polenta (cornmeal)
1 double handful milk or soya milk
1 handful unrefined sugar
1 banana
1 mango
1 handful canola oil
1 handful raisins

Note: 2 double handfuls liquid equals 250 ml, 8 fl oz or 1 cup

This is an exceptionally delicious dessert to serve at a party, or a yummy snack to enjoy between meals, accompanied by Yogi Tea (see p.26).

- Heat the oven to 180°C/350°F.
- Line the bottom of a rectangular cake tin (30x20x5 cm/13x9x2 in) with a sheet of oiled baking paper.
- Place all the ingredients in a food processor and blend to a smooth paste.
- Pour the batter into the prepared cake tin and place it on the middle rack of the oven.
- Bake for 31 minutes or until the top is golden brown and firm to the touch. You can also test if the cake is cooked by inserting a skewer into its centre – the skewer should come out clean.
- Completely cool the cake in the tin before turning out onto a plate.

Sat Nam

Ancient amaranth pudding delight

You will need
1 double handful amaranth
1 tin (450 ml/16 fl oz) coconut milk
1 small handful raisins
1 large apple, grated
peel (zest) of 1 orange, finely grated
1 handful honey
1 mudra pinch cinnamon

Amaranth, a highly nutritious grain, has a colourful history. It was a staple food of the pre-Columbian Aztecs who, believing it had supernatural powers, used it in their religious ceremonies.

Before the Spanish conquest in 1519, amaranth was associated with human sacrifice. The Aztec women made a mixture of ground amaranth and honey, or human blood, which they shaped into idols and ate ceremoniously. When the Spanish conquistadors came, they were so shocked by this practice they forbade the consumption of amaranth. The grain disappeared from the human diet for hundreds of years. Today it can be found in health food stores and some specialist food markets.

- Place the amaranth and coconut milk in a small pot and bring to the boil.
- Lower the heat and add the raisins, grated apple, orange peel, honey and cinnamon.
- Cover and simmer until all the liquid is absorbed and the amaranth has puffed up. This will take 11–15 minutes.
- Serve either warm or cold with fresh or baked fruit.

Sat Nam

Carob, banana and walnut cake

You will need

2 double handfuls canola oil
2 double handfuls date syrup or honey
1 double handful orange juice
2 handfuls carob powder
2 handfuls flax seeds (linseeds) purée (see below)
3 double handfuls wholemeal flour
1 mudra pinch baking powder
2 bananas, sliced
1 handful raisins
1 handful walnuts, roughly chopped

Note: 2 double handfuls liquid equals 250 ml, 8 fl oz or 1 cup

This is a rich cake that is great for both special occasions and everyday eating. It is often baked as a celebration at the end of yoga retreats or yogic gatherings. There is no dairy, no eggs and no sugar, so this is a healthy cake with no cholesterol – *Wha-hay Guroo* (all yogis smile).

The world over, Kundalini Yogis celebrate the solstice twice a year at the solstice equinox. Participants spend seven days camping, joining in on the many yoga classes, children's activities and other healing events that take place. The winter solstice is held in Orlando, Florida, and the summer solstice in Espanola, New Mexico. These are wonderful gatherings. If you are unable to attend a camp, bake this cake at home. Whilst this is not a traditional solstice recipe, it is symbolic of the spirit of the solstice gatherings.

As with the other recipes in this book, the ingredients for this cake are measured using your hands – baking free-style. After years of experience we can guarantee it works. The beauty of using hand measures is that the dish tastes a little different each time it is prepared. For those of you not comfortable with the idea of baking a cake free-style, refer to the measurement summary on page 24.

Before you start measuring, breathe deeply and rub your hands rapidly together to create *prana* – whatever you touch will be energised.

- Heat the oven to 200°C/400°F/gas mark 6.
- Place the canola oil, date syrup or honey, orange juice and carob powder in either a large glass bowl or a large food processor. If you use honey, the cake will be lighter in colour when cooked.
- Mix well, then add the flax seed purée (see below).
- Mix again, then add the wholemeal flour and baking powder. Beat quickly for 18 turns if you use a glass bowl. If you use a food processor, blend until you achieve a light, even consistency – you may need to transfer the ingredients to a large bowl at this stage.
- Add the sliced bananas, raisins and roughly chopped walnuts and fold through.
- Transfer the mixture into a lightly oiled and lined 24-cm (9-in) round cake tin.
- Place the tin in the pre-heated oven and bake for 10 minutes. Reduce the temperature to 180°C/350°F/gas mark 4 and bake for a further 21 minutes. To test if the cake is cooked, insert a skewer into its centre – the skewer should come out clean.
- Remove the cake from the oven. Cool in the tin for 11 minutes, then turn out onto a wire cake rack.
- Keep covered in the refrigerator for up to 4 days. Serve with Yogic Dessert Cream (see p. 119).
- **For the flax seed purée:** soak the flax seeds for 11 minutes in triple their amount of water. Place into a food processor and blend until the mixture is smooth and takes on a bubbly, white appearance.

Sat Nam

Yogic dessert cream

You will need
- 1 double handful hard coconut butter
- 1 double handful single (light) cream (variation)
- seeds from 1 vanilla pod
- 1 handful honey
- 1 mudra pinch grated lemon rind (zest)
- 1 mudra pinch grated orange rind (zest)

This is a delicious and versatile dessert cream that can be made plain or flavoured and coloured using different fruit. The Carob, Banana and Walnut Cake (see p. 118) tastes particularly good with mango or strawberry Yogic Dessert Cream.

- Place the coconut butter or cream, if using, seeds from the vanilla pod, honey, lemon rind and orange rind in a food processor.
- Blend until well combined.
- **For orange-flavoured Yogic Dessert Cream:** purée the flesh of 1 mango and blend through 1 portion of plain Yogic Dessert Cream.
- **For strawberry-flavoured Yogic Dessert Cream:** hull 1 handful of strawberries and purée. Blend through 1 portion of plain Yogic Dessert Cream.

Sat Nam

Carob, banana and walnut cake with strawberry-flavoured dessert cream

TOP LEFT Tofu yogic cheese (see p. 124)
BOTTOM LEFT Ang sang wha-hay guru mango chutney (see p. 124)
ABOVE Aubergine and sesame baba ganoush (see p. 125)
RIGHT Green chilli and garlic paste (see p. 124)

8 Food for women

Celebrating women through nourishing food

Women are inspiring, nurturing and complex human beings. Part of Kundalini Yoga is the belief in the power of the feminine principle – the *Shakti* – with an understanding that women embody the creative aspect of God, and that they have the power to create the prevailing values and spiritual consciousness of the world.

Yogi Bhajan always celebrated the power and grace of women, and he showed many women the way to access their own inherent qualities of vitality, radiance, inner strength and talent through Kundalini Yoga. Today, women's courses, camps and programmes continue to form a nucleus for women, from all walks of life all over the world, to renew and refresh themselves.

Women have a unique and complex biochemistry, and their bodies require different kinds of nurturing, during the different stages of their lives. From puberty to pregnancy, from child-bearing to menopause, a woman's body has different needs. The Kundalini Yoga Technology for Women is about creating a system for each woman to love the body she has, and to always enjoy the stage of life she is in. The key for a woman is self-love, and a positive way of expressing this self-love is to give her body the nutrients she needs to heal and nourish it. Both the authors of this book studied under Shakta Kaur Khalsa, a direct student of Yogi Bhajan since 1976. She is the embodiment of the 'face of a woman' that Yogi Bhajan spoke about so succinctly, and she has inspired us greatly. We are honoured to have been her students and have written this chapter with Shakta Kaur Khalsa in mind.

In Kundalini Yoga Technology there are 12 ingredients considered essential for women – all 12 are used extensively in the recipes in this chapter. You will also notice that we regularly cook with aubergine (eggplant). Its shape symbolises the fertility of a woman's body; it is low in saturated fats and cholesterol; and it is rich in vitamin B6 and copper. Although aubergine has a relatively high sodium content, it is too good a fruit, eaten as a vegetable, to be omitted – we simply don't cook it with salt.

Of the 12 items we recommend you take daily: one tablespoon of almond oil, the supreme of all oils, as it helps eliminate toxins; five soaked and peeled almonds, to keep impurities from building up in your body; one banana for potassium; and 10 raisins, for potassium, eaten around 4.00 p.m.

To help women bring these 'essentials' into their daily routine, and to enjoy a diet of maximum benefit, we recommend they start their day with a breakfast of orange, apple or mango juice, or almond milk with rice bran syrup; that they have their main meal at lunch time; and they eat a very light dinner – soups, salads and steamed vegetables are ideal.

ESSENTIALS FOR WOMEN

Almond oil – for healthy skin and hair; eliminates toxins
Aubergine – for hormone balance; energising
Ginger – for the nervous system
Green chilli (mild) – prevents constipation; for Vitamin C
Mango – corrects menstrual cycle irregularities
Rice bran syrup – a good source of B vitamins
Sesame oil – for female hormone imbalance
Turmeric – helps to heal internal organs
Wheatberries – cleanses the intestinal tract; nourishing
Yoghurt – helps cleans and heal the digestive system

Turnip fast

You will need
3 white turnips, washed

From the store cupboard
almond oil
freshly ground pepper
turmeric
tamari soy sauce

Turnips, with their high vitamin B6 content, are a good, natural way of addressing the discomforts associated with female hormone imbalance. Eat as much as you want, but keep it within a framework of three meals a day. Drink eight glasses of healing water each day, and drink Yogi Tea as you please (see p. 26). Mono-diets such as the Turnip Fast are kept for five, upto a maximum of ten, days.

Chanting the *Chatay Pad* mantra (see p. 155) gives inner peace and happiness, and encourages good fortune. It also helps develop intuition, clears the mind and purifies the conscious. The words invoke the various names of God to help bring about prosperity, peace of mind and the capacity to look beyond this world to realise the Infinite. Chant this whilst cooking.

- Take the turnips and place them in a steamer over a pot of simmering water. Steam until tender, then mash in a bowl. Add 3 swirls of almond oil, 1 small gyan pinch of freshly ground pepper and 1 small gyan pinch of turmeric.

Sat Nam

Yogi's mush diet

You will need
5 courgettes (zucchini), roughly sliced
4 celery sticks (stalks), roughly sliced
1 bunch fresh parsley
1 sprig fresh mint
1 small gyan pinch black pepper
cottage cheese

Yogi Bhajan recommended this 40-day diet for weight loss, skin beauty and cleansing the intestines. You can eat as much as you want of the following dish each day, but you must eat it no more than three times a day. In between meals you can drink Yogi Tea (see p. 26) and drink as much water as you like, but at least five glasses each day.

To infuse this dish with *prana*, we recommend you use your hands when mixing the ingredients. Whilst mixing, chant the mantra *Saa Taa Naa Maa* for 11 minutes. The vibration of your voice, and the love in your heart, will make this a truly yogic dish. It is a powerful mantra, and chanting it is a powerful catalyst for changing your life.

- Place the courgettes, celery sticks, parsley and mint in a bamboo steamer. Steam for 11–15 minutes, or until the vegetables are tender.
- Add the black pepper, then chanting *Saa Taa Naa Maa*, mush the vegetables and herbs with your hands for 11 minutes. Alternatively, purée in a food processor.
- Serve with cottage cheese when on the Yogi's Mush Diet.

Sat Nam

Wheatberries diet

You will need
1 double handful wheatberries
4 double handfuls healing water (see p. 25)

Sweet version
honey
milk or soya milk
cinnamon

Savoury version
2–4 tablespoons ghee
1 small gyan pinch turmeric
1 onion, diced
4 cloves garlic, finely diced
1 finger-length nub fresh ginger root, grated
1 gyan pinch black pepper
tamari soy sauce
sea salt

Note: 2 double handfuls liquid equals 250 ml, 8 fl oz and 1 cup

Yogi Bhajan recommended this diet to enhance the beauty of the woman – for skin that shines like gold; to build strong gums and teeth; to help with back and intestinal problems; and to reduce, to a minimum, the painful effects of the menopause. Do this diet for one day each week, eating as much as you like, but keeping to three meals.

For the sweet version

- Soak the wheatberries in 4 double handfuls of fresh water overnight.
- Drain, then steam or boil until soft – this will take approximately 1 hour. If using the boiling method, drain again once cooked.
- Add 1 swirl of honey and 2 swirls of milk or soya milk. Dust with a sprinkling of cinnamon.

For the savoury version

- Soak 3 handfuls of wheatberries in 3 double handfuls of fresh water overnight.
- Drain the wheatberries, then cook them in 6 double handfuls of water until they puff up and are soft – this will take approximately 1 hour. Drain.
- In the meantime, heat the ghee in a frying pan over a medium heat. Add the turmeric and cook for a couple of minutes. Next, add the onion, garlic and ginger. Combine well, then cook until the onion is tender.
- Add the prepared wheatberries and the black pepper. Season with tamari or sea salt.

Sat Nam

Tofu yogic cheese

You will need
1 block (450 g/1 lb) soft tofu
3 garlic cloves, finely diced
1 handful fresh basil leaves
1 handful fresh mint

From the store cupboard
olive oil
tamari soy sauce
apple cider vinegar

(pictured on page 120)

If you are a lover of cheese, this is a very healthy alternative for cream cheese. The garlic and herbs make it very tasty and provide a purifying effect. Change the ingredients as you wish, to taste. Tofu Yogi Cheese will keep for up to seven days in the refrigerator.

- Take the soft tofu and steam it over simmering water in a bamboo steamer for 5 minutes. Set aside to cool.
- Mash the cooled, lightly steamed tofu with a fork in a bowl to make a smooth paste. Alternatively, blend in a food processor.
- Add the garlic, basil and mint, 2 swirls of olive oil, 1 swirl of tamari and 7 drops of apple cider vinegar. Blend all the ingredients together. Season, to taste.

Sat Nam

Ang sang wha-hay guru mango chutney

You will need
2 medium tomatoes, diced
1 mango, peeled and diced
1 small red onion, diced
2 garlic cloves, chopped
juice of 1 lime
1 green chilli, de-seeded and diced

(pictured on page 120)

For women, the mango is the queen of all fruit, because of its soothing energies that are connected with the moon energies. This chutney is delicious with salads, rice and on its own on bread. Adjust the 'heat' of the chutney to your own taste and level of tolerance. Whilst the ingredients are blending, energise yourself by chanting *Ang Sang Wahe Guru* – 'The dynamic, living ecstasy of the Universe is dancing within every cell of me'.

- Place the diced tomatoes, mango and onion into a food processor, along with the garlic and lime juice. Add the diced chilli, to taste. Blend until thoroughly combined, but not too smooth. Keep covered in the refrigerator for up to 1 week.

Sat Nam

Green chilli and garlic paste

You will need
4–5 handfuls small green chillies
3 garlic cloves
juice of 1 lemon
1 handful fresh coriander (cilantro), chopped

(pictured on page 120)

The green chilli contains a high level of vitamin C, which acts as an antioxidant, and chlorophyll, which contains high levels of *prana*. This paste is meant to have a real punch, but you can adjust the recommended number of chillies to your own level of tolerance for hot and spicy foods.

- Purée, to a very fine paste, the whole chillies and garlic in a food processor.
- Add the lemon juice and transfer to a glass bowl.
- Add the chopped fresh coriander and mix thoroughly.
- Store in a covered container in the refrigerator for up to 4 weeks.
- Spread on bread, add to soups or serve with salads.

Sat Nam

Aubergine and sesame baba ganoush

You will need
1 aubergine (eggplant)
juice of 1 lemon
2 garlic cloves, finely chopped
2 mudra pinches fresh parsley leaves

From the store cupboard
tahini paste
olive oil
tamari soy sauce

(pictured on page 120)

Kundalini yogis use a lot of aubergine in their cooking, as it is highly nutritious for women, being both energising and excellent for hormone balance – its shape also honours womanhood. Whilst making this dish, chant the *Adi Shakti* mantra (see p. 155) to celebrate the importance of women at all stages of their lives. As Yogi Bhajan said, 'You can judge the strength of a nation by the face of a woman.'

- Heat the oven to 200°C/400°F/gas mark 6.
- Pierce the aubergine with a fork before placing it into the pre-heated oven.
- Cook the aubergine until it feels soft to touch. This will take approximately 22 minutes. Alternatively, carefully char the skin of the aubergine over an open flame.
- Carefully remove the aubergine from the oven and place it in a sealed plastic bag for 11 minutes. This is to allow it to steam and cook further.
- Remove the aubergine from the plastic bag. Holding it under running water, peel off the skin.
- Dice and place in a glass bowl. Using a spoon or fork, mash the aubergine with 2 spoonfuls of tahini paste, the lemon juice and garlic. Mix well, tracing the outline of the infinity symbol as you stir. Adjust the amount of tahini paste, to taste. Season with tamari.
- Scoop the mixture into a serving bowl. Garnish with 1 swirl of olive oil and the parsley leaves.
- Serve with rice or with pitta bread and salad for lunch, or as a snack with crudités at parties.

Sat Nam

Golden milk

You will need
1 generous sprinkle turmeric powder
2 spoonfuls healing water (see p. 25)
honey
2 large spoonfuls almond oil
2 double handfuls milk
2 double handfuls almond milk (variation)
cinnamon, freshly grated (optional)

Note: 2 double handfuls liquid equals 250 ml, 8 fl oz or 1 cup

This classic drink is from Yogi Bhajan, and is especially beneficial for women. The almond oil nourishes and lubricates the joints and the spine, whilst the turmeric warms-up the body and keeps it moving effortlessly.

Traditionally Golden Milk is made with dairy milk. Here, we have also suggested almond milk as a highly nutritious alternative.

- Boil the water and turmeric powder in a small saucepan for 8 minutes.
- In another saucepan, bring the almond oil and almond milk to the boil. Once boiling, remove from heat.
- Combine the water and milk mixtures. Add honey, to taste.
- Sprinkle with freshly grated nutmeg just before drinking – this adds a wonderful, aromatic taste (optional).

Sat Nam

Chickpea parmigiana with coriander sauce

You will need

2 aubergines (eggplants), sliced
1 double handful cooked chickpeas
2 garlic cloves, chopped
1 red onion, chopped
1 thumb-length nub fresh ginger root, finely chopped
grated rind (zest) of 1 lemon
juice of 1 lemon
1 handful fresh coriander (cilantro), chopped

From the store cupboard

cayenne pepper
olive oil
cider vinegar
ground coriander
green olives
freshly ground black pepper

Serves 2 to 4 persons

Parmigiana is an Italian dish and this is inspired by Signora Castellino of Turin, Italy. Signora Castellino is a practising doctor, mother of four children and a grandmother. She is radiant, graceful and bountiful – the embodiment of a Kundalini woman.

- Slice the aubergines into circles about 1 finger-width thick. Sprinkle with cayenne pepper, and brush with olive oil.
- Heat a heavy skillet or frying pan until very hot. Char the aubergine until soft on the inside and slightly burnt on the outside.
- Transfer the aubergine into a glass bowl and marinate in 2 spoonfuls of cider vinegar.
- Coarsely chop the chickpeas and place in a glass bowl. Add 1 mudra pinch of ground coriander, 1 crushed garlic clove, the onion, ginger, lemon rind and juice, and 10 green olives, stoned and chopped. Combine well, then set aside.
- Line a serving plate with 1 slice of aubergine. Top with a layer of the chickpea mixture, then another layer of aubergine. Finish with a layer of chickpea mixture. Create a higher stack if you want to serve bigger portions. Repeat based on the number of people eating.
- Serve with the Coriander Sauce (see below) drizzled on the top.
- **For the Coriander Sauce:** whiz in a food processor 4 tablespoons of olive oil, 1 chopped garlic clove and 1 handful of chopped fresh coriander until well-combined. Season to taste with freshly ground black pepper.

Sat Nam

Wha-hay lunch plate

You will need
1 packet (50 g/1¾ oz) wakame seaweed
1 double handful soya milk or milk
2 small aubergine
fresh breadcrumbs, made from 2 slices of bread
fresh coriander (cilantro) (for garnish)

From the store cupboard
dried mint
dried basil
arrowroot (or agar powder)
tamari soy sauce
flaked almonds (for garnish)

One of the many reasons why Yogi Bhajan recommends aubergine for women is because it energises the whole anatomical system and helps to regulate the menstrual flow – so this dish is a very powerful dish for women. As a version of pakoras, a classic Punjabi snack, it includes almonds – almond oil being one of Kundalini Yoga's 'essentials for women' (see p. 122) – and seaweed, which is a rich source of iron and vitamin B12.

- Heat the oven to 200°C/400°F/gas mark 6.
- Soak the wakame seaweed in hot water until soft. Drain and set aside.
- Make a batter for the aubergine. Place in a glass bowl the soya milk or milk, 1 small gyan pinch each of dried mint, dried basil and arrowroot (or the agar powder, if using), and 1 splash of tamari. Whisk until well combined.
- Peel and slice the aubergine into circles about 1 finger-width thick.
- Dip the aubergine into the batter, then roll each piece in the breadcrumbs.
- Place on an oiled baking sheet, then bake in the pre-heated oven for 22 minutes, or until brown and crispy.
- Take the drained wakame seaweed and place it on a serving platter, creating a bed for the aubergine.
- Arrange the aubergine circles on top of the seaweed.
- To serve, sprinkle generously with the flaked almonds and the chopped fresh coriander.

Sat Nam

Khalsa lentil soup

You will need
1 large onion, diced
3 garlic cloves, crushed
1 thumb-length nub fresh ginger root, finely grated
1 handful yellow lentils, washed and soaked overnight
2 parsnips, peeled and cut into chunks
2–3 carrots, peeled and cut into chunks

From the store cupboard
olive oil
ground cumin
bay leaves
healing water (see p. 25)
freshly ground black pepper

Khalsa means pure, and the Khalsas are Sikhs who have undergone the sacred Amrit Ceremony, initiated by Guru Gobind Singh. Today, the Khalsa family, many of European descent, embraces members from around the world, united by a common path. This soup is very warming, and is symbolic of both the friendships between women and the friendships made within the Kundalini Yoga family.

- Warm a couple of swirls of olive oil in a large saucepan and sauté the onion, ginger and garlic. Combine with the drained lentils, parsnips, carrots, 3 mudra pinches ground cumin and 2 bay leaves.
- Fill the saucepan with healing water to approximately 2 cm (¾ in) above the lentils and vegetables. Bring to the boil, then turn the heat down and simmer. Cook until the lentils and vegetables are tender. Take off the heat and cool slightly.
- Remove the bay leaves, transfer to a food processor and blend until the consistency is that of a medium-to-thick soup.
- Season with freshly ground black pepper, to taste.

Sat Nam

Wha-hay guroo aubergine salad

You will need
2 aubergines (eggplants)
1 tiny red chilli, de-seeded and finely chopped
juice of 1 lemon
coriander leaves (cilantro), chopped

From the store cupboard
olive oil
freshly ground black pepper
sesame seeds

This dish is a gift from Chloe Morris that has raw aubergine as its main ingredient – we were all shocked, surprised and sceptical. After all, the most common way to cook aubergine is to leave it covered in salt, especially unhealthy for women, and then to fry it in oil, which is bad for the heart. Chloe showed us how to hand-ripen the aubergine by using our hands to massage in the olive oil, imbuing it with our energies. This we did as we chanted the *Guru Mantra of Ecstacy* (see p. 155). The result was a heavenly dish.

- Cut the aubergines into fine strips and place in a large bowl.
- Pour in some olive oil and gently massage, adding more oil, as required. The aubergines should turn soft and a pale golden colour. Don't forget to chant *Wha-hay Guroo, Wha-hey Guroo, Wha-hay Guroo. Wha-hay Jeeo* whilst doing this.
- Mix through the chopped chilli, then season with freshly ground black pepper, to taste.
- This dish can be served immediately, but it tastes best after it has been left to marinate overnight.
- To serve, squeeze the lemon juice on the aubergine and toss through. Sprinkle with chopped coriander leaves and 1 mudra pinch of sesame seeds.

Sat Nam

TOP Khalsa lentil soup
BOTTOM Wha-hay guroo aubergine salad

Tofu, aubergine and pepper baked pastry

You will need
1 aubergine
1 block (450 g/1 lb) tofu
1 packet (450 g/1 lb) puff pastry
juice of 1 lemon
1 red (sweet) pepper, sliced
1 red onion, sliced
7 leaves fresh basil, chopped

From the store cupboard
olive oil
tamari soy sauce
sesame seeds

Traditionally, yogis eat this dish for brunch or lunch, but it is also a great dish to serve at parties. Whilst the pastry is baking, you may like to learn the *Guru Gaitri* mantra (see p. 155). This mantra brings about stability to both the left and right hemispheres of the brain. It also works on the heart-centre to help develop compassion, patience and tolerance, uniting you with the Infinite.

- Heat the oven to 200°C/400°F/gas mark 6.
- Peel the aubergine. Cut it in half, then cut each half into 3 wedges. Rub a few drops of olive oil into each wedge. Set aside.
- Cut the tofu into finger-width slices. Marinate for 15 minutes in equal amounts of tamari and lemon juice. Place the tofu on an oiled baking sheet and cook in the oven for 11 minutes.
- Whilst the tofu is baking, roll out the puff pastry into a 30x20-cm (12x8-in) rectangle on a floured surface. Slice the red pepper and red onion into fine strips.
- Layer the red pepper and onion, the aubergine and the baked tofu on the puff pastry, leaving a 3-cm (1¾-in) gap along all the edges. Sprinkle the chopped basil and 1 mudra pinch of sesame seeds on the filling. Roll up the pastry, tucking in the sides as you do so.
- Sprinkle generously with more sesame seeds. Bake for 31–35 minutes.
- Whilst the pastry is baking, use the time to learn the *Guru Gaitri* mantra.

Sat Nam

Women guru curry

You will need
1 onion, diced
4 garlic cloves, crushed
1 thumb-length nub fresh ginger root, finely chopped
1 handful chickpea flour
juice of 1 lemon
1 heaped spoonful yoghurt
2 handfuls almonds, blanched and peeled
1 handful walnuts
2 mudra pinches pumpkin seeds
2 courgettes (zucchini), sliced
2 carrots, sliced
1 green chilli, finely chopped
1 bunch fresh coriander (cilantro), chopped

From the store cupboard
healing water (see p. 25)
turmeric
tamari soy sauce

This recipe is a straight adaptation from the ancient Vedic scriptures, where it states, 'Oh woman, if you can prepare this kind of food, and just live on it, it will be a splendid idea, and nobody will know why you are so beautiful and great.'

- Sauté the onion, garlic and ginger with a few drops of healing water in a large frying pan until soft. Add more water, if required, to stop any burning and to ensure the trinity of vegetables sauté in their own juices.
- When soft, add the chickpea flour, lemon juice and 1 mudra pinch of turmeric. Mix well, tracing the outline of the infinity symbol as you stir.
- To obtain a creamy texture, add 1 heaped spoonful of yoghurt. Mix for a further 3 minutes over a medium heat.
- Add the blanched almonds, walnuts, pumpkin seeds, sliced courgettes and carrots, chopped green chilli and coriander. Continue to stir until heated through. Add tamari soy sauce, to taste.
- Serve with rice, chapatti (see p. 100) and salad.

Sat Nam

Shakti majestic fruit salad

You will need

1 peach
1 plum
1 persimmon, skinned
1 papaya (pawpaw), de-seeded and peeled
1 fig
1 pear
1 guava
1 banana
seeds of 1 pomegranate
1 mango
4 fresh dates
juice of 1 orange

For this fruit salad we picked fresh fruits that are especially nutritious for women. Of course, you don't need to use them all – pick and choose from our selection to make your own special dish. Feel free to change the quantities of each fruit used, to taste. Since this majestic fruit salad is so good for you, eat as much as you like, but remember it is best to eat fruit on an empty stomach. This will ensure you digest the fruit properly and that you absorb maximum nutrients from the fruit. It will also prevent problems such as bloating and constipation. The woman is the *Shakti* energy, the lunar side of the Universe that is both nourishing and calming. This salad celebrates the richness of a woman's soul.

- Cut all the fruit, except the pomegranate, into little cubes and place in a large glass bowl – it is best not to use a metal bowl, as the metal abuses the vitamins in the fruit.
- Seed the pomegranate and add the seeds to the diced fruit selection.
- Pour over the orange juice and toss through using your hands.
- This fruit salad will keep in the refrigerator for up to 1 day, but the sooner it is eaten, after making, the more nutritious it will be.

Sat Nam

Vegetable salad with kundalini dressing

You will need
1 iceberg lettuce
1 small bunch fresh basil leaves
4 handfuls baby salad greens
2 tomatoes, finely diced
1 small cucumber, diced
1 small bunch radish, diced
juice of 1 lemon
1 small handful toasted sesame seeds

From the store cupboard
balsamic vinegar
olive oil
sesame oil
tamari soy sauce

This salad is served with a wonderful Kundalini, women-inspired dressing – strong, cosmopolitan and beautiful. To maximise its goodness, and so that it absorbs all the flavours, let the vegetables marinate in the Kundalini Dressing for at least 22 minutes.

- Tear the iceberg lettuce and basil leaves using your hands. Mix them with the baby salad greens in a large salad bowl.
- Add the diced tomatoes, cucumber and radish.
- Pour on the Kundalini Dressing (see below) and toss through. Use your hands to do this to transfer your *prana* on to the food.
- Let the salad marinate for at least 22 minutes before serving.
- **For the Kundalini Dressing:** mix together the lemon juice, 1 swirl of balsamic vinegar, 2 swirls of olive oil, a few dashes of sesame oil, 7 drops of tamari and the toasted sesame seeds.

Sat Nam

Aubergine and pomegranate soup

You will need
1 onion, diced
7 cloves garlic, finely chopped
2 aubergines (eggplants), peeled and diced
juice of 7 pomegranates
juice of 1 lemon
2 mudra pinches chopped fresh parsley

From the store cupboard
healing water (see p. 25)
yogic or organic stock (bouillon) cube (see p. 27)
olive oil
sea salt

Note: 2 double handfuls liquid equals 250 ml, 8 fl oz and 1 cup

This soup, originally a Syrian recipe, has been adapted for the yogic diet – one without meat. It goes well with rice and cooked soya beans. The lemon flavour comes from the pomegranate juice, which is a good cleanser for the blood.

- Dry-fry the onion and garlic in a large saucepan, over a medium heat, until soft but not brown. Add the aubergine and the pomegranate juice.
- Pour in enough healing water to half fill the saucepan.
- Crumble in 1 stock cube and add 2 swirls of olive oil. Bring to the boil, then reduce the heat and simmer for 31 minutes.
- Add sea salt and lemon juice, to taste.
- Serve with a sprinkling of freshly chopped parsley.

Sat Nam

Humee hum brahm hum soup

You will need
2 courgettes (zucchini), sliced into thick circles
2 carrots, peeled and diced
1 beetroot (beet), diced
1 onion, diced
1 potato, diced
1 broccoli head, broken into florets
4 garlic cloves, crushed
1–2 small green chillies, de-seeded and chopped

From the store cupboard
healing water (see p. 25)
yogic stock or organic (bouillon) stock cube (see p. 27)
turmeric
tamari soy sauce

Literally, the mantra *Humee Hum Brahm Hum* means we are the spirit of God – the total spirit. In this soup, each of the different vegetables represents a Self; together they represent the total spirit. This mantra fixes the identity into its true reality.

In the Kundalini Yoga diet, it is recommended for women to have one meal of steamed vegetables each day. This is best eaten for dinner, three hours before going to bed. We prepared this soup as a delicious and very healthy low-fat alternative. Whilst cooking, remember to chant, full of expression, *Humee Hum Brahm Hum*.

- Place all the vegetables, except the green chilli, in a bamboo steamer. Steam until tender.
- Whilst the vegetables are steaming, pour healing water into a saucepan until half full and bring to the boil.
- Chop the chilli and add to the water, adjusting the quantity used to taste. Add 1 stock cube and 1 gyan pinch of turmeric.
- When cooked, place the steamed vegetable in the boiling water. Stir once, using a circular motion. Add tamari, to taste.

Sat Nam

9 Yoga and friends

Growing group consciousness

Doing yoga with friends is a very powerful experience – not only are you personally working on your own awakening but also, together, you are building group consciousness. These gatherings are called *satsang* and they form a key part of the yogic path. *Satsang* literally means 'in the company of the wise', and they are a time when ideals and principles of truth are discussed. The focus of these discourses ranges from spiritual life, health and healing to emotional health, attachment, desire, dreams and spiritual experience to evolution, reincarnation, world affairs, ashram life and the world beyond.

As with any undertaking, however, cultivating a yogic way of life begins with you, and *sadhana*, or personal practice, is one of the fundamentals of Kundalini Yoga. A *sadhana* is a commitment – it is a relationship with one's Self. Whilst there are guidelines, the underlying principle is to do something every day. This can be a two-and-a-half-hour *sadhana*; an eleven-minute meditation; or a yoga class or yoga routine completed at home. It is the practice of connecting with your spirit, getting to know your Inner Self and experiencing the joy that lies deep within you. In the Kundalini Yoga tradition, it is suggested that *sadhana* is done early in the morning, in the ambrosial hour between 4.00 am and 7.00 am, as this is seen as the optimum time for spiritual practice. It also prepares you for the day ahead.

In this chapter we include a number of kriyas and meditations that can form the foundations of your *sadhana*, and can also be practised with friends when they come round to share your food. We also explain a number of mudras, which you can use during your practice, and are the basis for measuring ingredients in this book.

Tuning in and warm-up session

The first thing you do before a Kundalini Yoga session or meditation is to 'tune in' to your Inner Wisdom. Tuning in is the chanting of the *Adi* mantra in a very specific way. It is considered to be a vital introduction to any practice in order to complete a link with the great teachers and avatars, who provide protection and guidance during the practice.

After tuning in it is necessary to spend a few minutes warming up. Here we provide two exercises you can do. In Kundalini Yoga, to give deeper impact to our actions, we mentally chant *Sat* on the inhale and *Nam* on the exhale. As you do this concentrate on the third eye, which is the point between the eyebrows.

TUNING IN

Every Kundalini Yoga practice is preceded by tuning in with the *Adi* Mantra (see p. 155). To begin, sit quietly in Easy Pose (see below) with your eyes closed and your spine straight; or if you prefer, use any other meditation pose that you may find more comfortable. Focusing your attention on your breath, centre yourself by breathing slowly in long, deep breaths for a few minutes. Do this until you feel calm and ready to commence your practice.

When ready, bring your palms and fingers together in the *Prayer Mudra* at your heart centre. Your fingers should be pointing 60 degrees upwards and outwards from your chest, with the sides and base of your thumbs pressing against your sternum.

Still with your eyes closed, focus on both your third eye and your heart centre. Inhale deeply, then chant *Ong Namo* as you exhale. The *Ong*, a long sound relative to *Namo*, should vibrate in the back of your throat and the cranium and nasal passages. Ideally the *Adi Mantra* is chanted on the one out breath. If this is not possible, pause here and take a short inhale before continuing with *Guroo Dayv Namo* – the *Guroo* is short; the *Dayv* is extended; the *Na* is short and the *Mo* completes the breath.

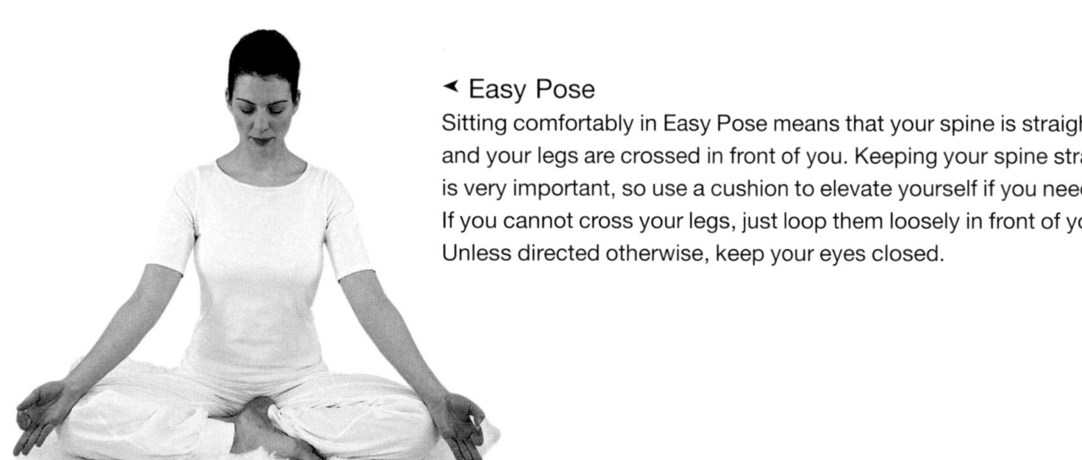

◄ Easy Pose
Sitting comfortably in Easy Pose means that your spine is straight and your legs are crossed in front of you. Keeping your spine straight is very important, so use a cushion to elevate yourself if you need to. If you cannot cross your legs, just loop them loosely in front of you. Unless directed otherwise, keep your eyes closed.

▲ Cat-Cow

Kneel on all fours on the ground. Your hands should be directly beneath your shoulders and your knees should be shoulder-width apart directly below your hips.

Inhale and arch your back in a curve downwards – raise your face up towards the ceiling as you do this. Feel the extension in your spine. This is called the Cow pose.

Next, exhale and draw your body upwards in an arch as high as you can. Keep your hands and knees on the ground, and flex your neck so that your head points to the ground. This is called the Cat pose.

Repeat the Cat-Cow movement for 3 minutes. To finish, inhale deeply and hold the Cow pose for 10 seconds.

➤ Leg Stretch

Sit on the floor with your legs stretched out in front of you and your arms by your sides.

Inhale and raise your arms towards the ceiling, keeping them straight.

Exhale and lower your torso and arms in a straight line down towards your toes, stretching from the pelvis. If you are able to, grab hold of your toes with both your thumbs and your two first fingers.

Stay in this position, inhaling and exhaling. On each exhale, relax further forwards, lowering your navel towards your legs. Feel your 'life nerve' (sciatic) stretch and expand. Continue for 3 minutes.

To finish, inhale and stretch further forwards, holding this position for 10 seconds. Exhale and slowly return to the starting position.

You are now ready for your practice – complete a kriya, relax and then meditate. If you wish, you can use appropriate mantra music to accompany your practice, as specified by Yogi Bhajan (see p. 160, Resources), otherwise practise in silence. When you conclude your Kundalini Yoga practice chant three long *Sat Nams*.

The mudras

The fingers and thumbs are where the *nadis*, or energy channels, in your body end. By placing subtle pressures on these points, you are communicating with your mind and body. A mudra is a hand position used in yoga, and is created by locking your fingers in a particular position, with the effect of guiding energy flow to different parts of the brain. Where the energy flows to depends on the point of contact between the fingers and the thumbs.

The mudras we chose to include in this book are those that you can easily use when cooking and serving food. The *Gurprasaad Mudra*, *Praying Mantis Mudra* and *Gyan Mudra* are also the standard tools used to measure the ingredients (see p. 23).

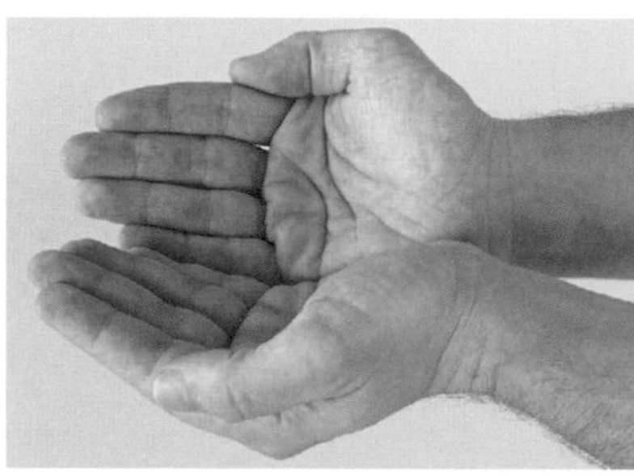

Gurprasaad Mudra
Cup your hands holding the sides of your palms and little fingers together. This mudra is the gift of the guru to receive the blessings for health, wealth and happiness.

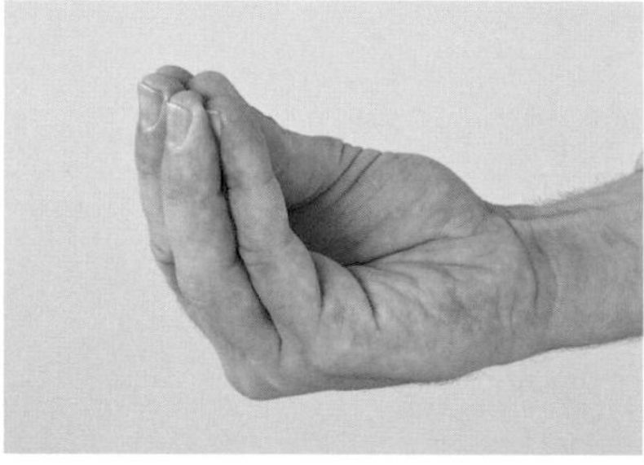

Praying Mantis Mudra
Join the tips of all your fingers together with the tip of your thumb. This mudra is for focus and the blending of the five elements (earth, ether, air, fire and water) in harmony.

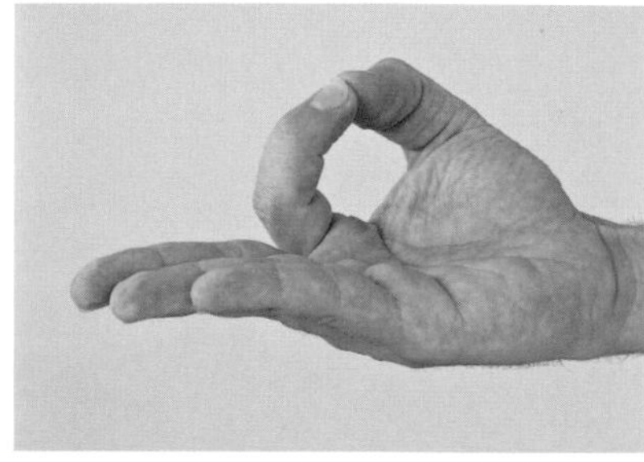

Gyan Mudra
Join the tip of your first finger with the tip of your thumb. This is the receptive mudra for knowledge and divine wisdom, linking the energy of Earth to Jupiter.

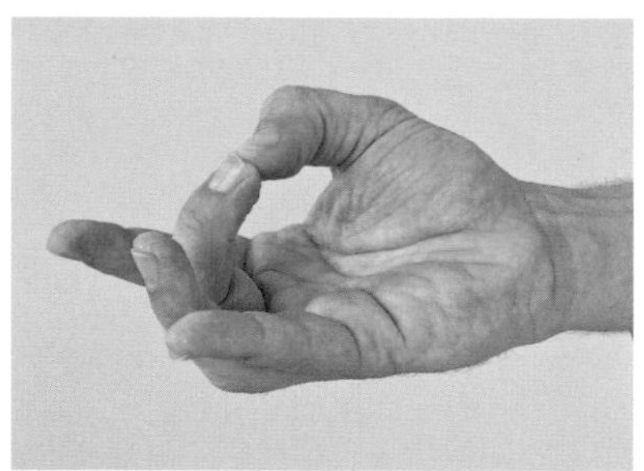

Shuni Mudra
Join the tip of your second finger with the tip of your thumb – keep your other fingers as straight as possible. This mudra brings the energy of Saturn to Earth, to facilitate patience and to channel emotional devotion.

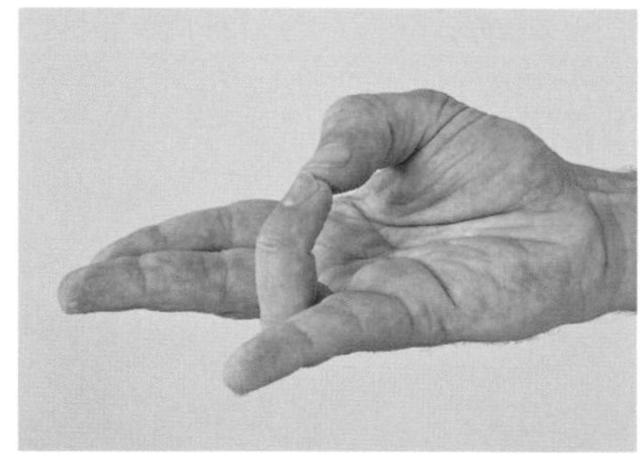

Surya Mudra
Join the tip of your third finger and the tip of your thumb. This brings the energies of the Sun and Venus to Earth, for physical health, vitality and beauty.

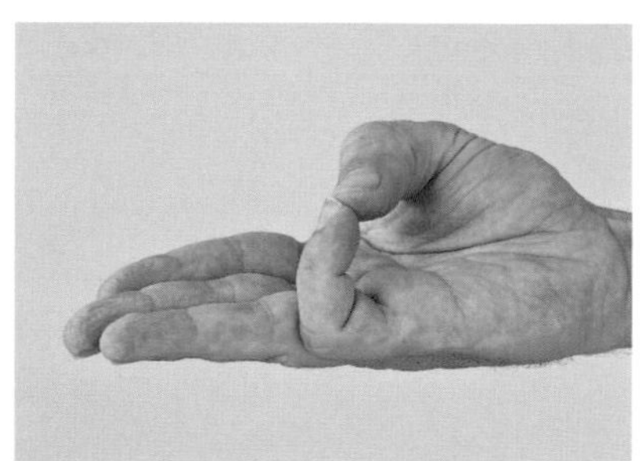

Buddhi Mudra
Join the tip of your little finger and your thumb. This links the energies of Mercury and Earth, to facilitate faster communication and healing.

THE FIVE ELEMENTS

In Ayurvedic medicine (see pp. 20–21), the physical body of human beings is made up of the five elements, or *tattva*, of the natural world – earth, water, fire, air and ether – and each element connects to a 'projection' or emotion – earth projects grit, water projects lust, fire projects anger, air projects attachment and ether projects pride and the ego.

The five elements continuously transmute into each other, and for human beings, they transmute into the three vital energies, or *doshas*, known as *Vata*, *Pitta* and *Kapha* that are responsible for all the physical and psychological aspects of the body and the mind. Each of these *doshas* have a dominant, or primary, element – the dominant element of *Vata* is air, with ether as its secondary element; the dominant element of *Pitta* is fire, with water as its secondary element; and the dominant element of *Kapha* is water, with air as its secondary element.

In Kundalini Yoga, through the practice of kriyas and meditations, and by using specific mudras, the connection of each element and its projection can be balanced and harmonised, helping you to achieve pure health in both body and mind.

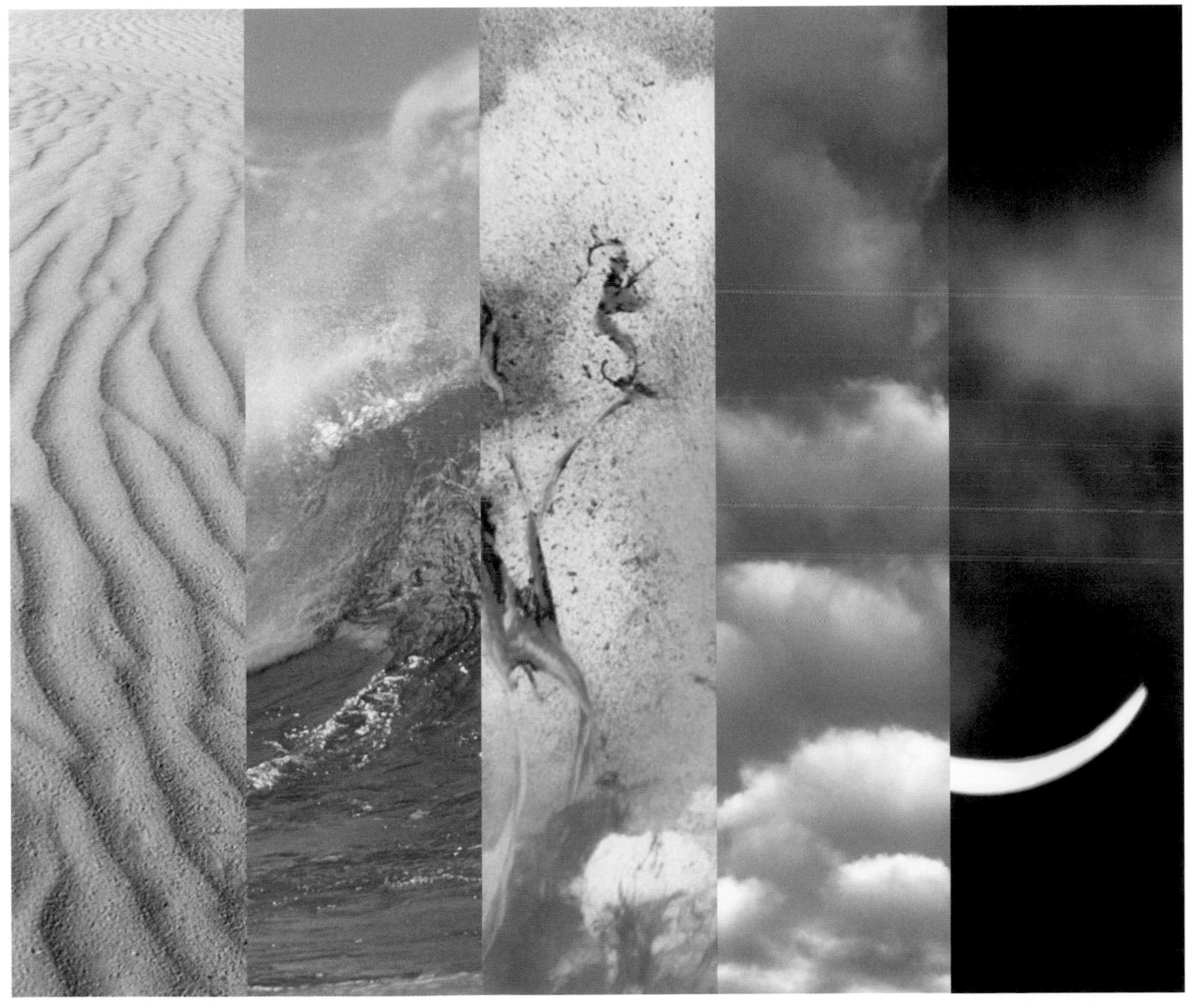

The kriyas

Whilst the word kriya means action, in Kundalini Yoga it is a sequence of breaths, postures and sounds that are incorporated in a specific way for a specific reason. Though it implies doing something, in its deepest sense it goes beyond the physical – doing a kriya is a commitment to see a particular state of being become a reality. Through kriyas, the seeds of our intentions bloom into actuality, and mastering a kriya brings about a sense of grace, power and the ability to complete things. Kriya is Kundalini Technology and, as a kriya is more than a random sequence of events, each one must be performed accurately according to the instructions as given by Yogi Bhajan.

DETOXIFICATION KRIYA

Detoxification, as taught by Yogi Bhajan on 29 May 1984

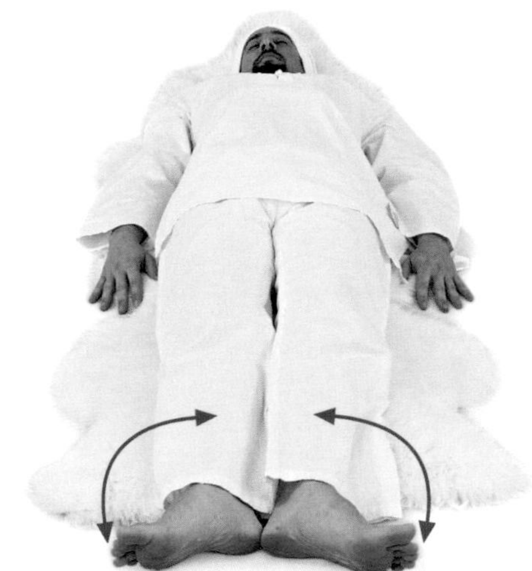

➤ Lie flat on your back with your legs straight. Bring your feet as close to the ground as possible, and place your heels together. Turn your toes outwards – flex your left foot to the left and your right foot to the right (see right).

Bring your toes together so that they are parallel and point up, and with the inside edges of your feet touching. Repeat this action of opening and closing your feet for 4 minutes. Ensure your heels remain together at all times.

▲ Next, rest your hands behind your head. Raise both your legs so that your feet are 60 cm (2 ft) above the ground. Move each leg up and down rapidly in a scissor motion, as if you are cutting a piece of paper. Ensure that the descending heel does not touch the ground, and both legs remain straight at all times. Do this for 4 minutes. When performed vigorously, this action clears away inner anger.

◄ Now roll over and lie on your stomach with your arms bent and hands beside your head. Stick out your tongue. Exhale and raise your chest off the ground, lifting your torso into the Cobra Pose – push from your chest and not from your lower back or buttocks. Inhale and lower your torso back to the ground. Repeat with strong breaths for 6½ minutes. This is a good detoxification exercise.

► Turn over and lie on your back with your arms by your sides. Draw your knees to your chest and raise your arms straight up, palms facing inwards and arms parallel to each other. Next, keeping your arms parallel to your body and your legs straight, lower your arms and legs back down towards the floor simultaneously. Repeat for 3 minutes in a controlled and conscious manner. Ensure your arms and legs touch the floor silently each time they are lowered.

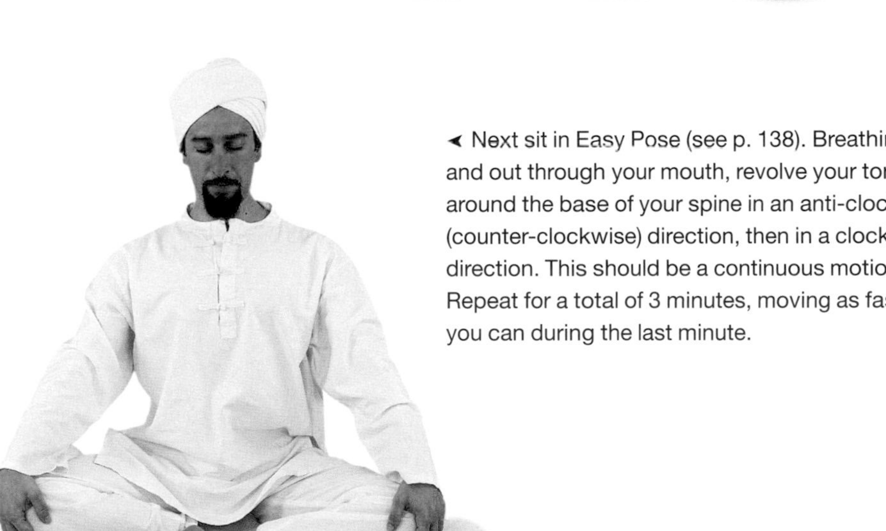

◄ Next sit in Easy Pose (see p. 138). Breathing in and out through your mouth, revolve your torso around the base of your spine in an anti-clockwise (counter-clockwise) direction, then in a clockwise direction. This should be a continuous motion. Repeat for a total of 3 minutes, moving as fast as you can during the last minute.

▲ Come to standing. Bend down and grab your ankles, keeping your legs straight. Hold onto your ankles, then lower yourself into a squat position with your buttocks hovering just above the ground – keep your feet flat on the floor, if possible. Come back to standing, still holding your ankles. Do this movement, the Crow Squat, for 2 minutes.

▲ Return to Easy Pose and chant *Sat Naam, Sat Naam, Sat Naam, Sat Naam, Sat Naam, Sat Naam, Wha-hay Guroo* for 11 minutes. Each repetition of the mantra takes 7–8 seconds.

◄ To finish, inhale deeply and stretch your arms straight above your head with your palms touching. Hold your breath for 20–40 seconds, lengthening your spine as much as you can. Repeat 2 more times, then exhale and relax your hands, arms and shoulders.

HEALING THE STOMACH KRIYA

Healing of the stomach (to aid digestion), as taught by Yogi Bhajan on 15 May 1985

▲ Sit in Easy Pose (see p. 138), stretch your arms out to your sides with your palms facing upwards – keep your arms straight and at shoulder level. Feel the stretch at the elbows. Your head should be kept level on your neck in a neutral position throughout the kriya. Open your mouth, then stick out your tongue slightly and roll it. Breathe in and out heavily through your rolled tongue.

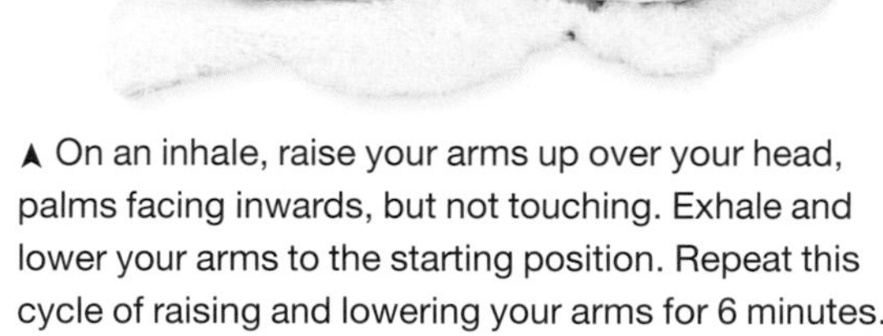

▲ On an inhale, raise your arms up over your head, palms facing inwards, but not touching. Exhale and lower your arms to the starting position. Repeat this cycle of raising and lowering your arms for 6 minutes.

◄ Next, grab your shoulders with your fingertips. Continue breathing through your rolled tongue. Inhale and twist your torso to the left, then exhale and twist your torso to the right. Continue this movement for 2 minutes.

▲ Return to Easy Pose (or Lotus Position if you can) and grab your knees with your hands. Still breathing through your rolled tongue, inhale and roll backwards. Exhale, come back up to sitting, and continue to roll forwards bringing your forehead to the ground. Rise and roll backwards on the in breath, then roll forwards again on the out breath. Do this for 3 minutes.

➤ Next, raise your arms to form a 'V' shape above you, palms facing upwards, as if you are receiving blessings. Concentrate on your third eye, the spot between and slightly above your eyebrows. Breathe slowly and deeply through your rolled tongue for 4 minutes.

a

b

▲➤ Return to the starting position, with both arms extended straight out to your sides at shoulder level, palms facing upwards (see p. 145). Raise your arms to a 45-degree angle to your body (a), then rotate them so your palms face downwards.

Lower your arms until your arms are at shoulder level (b), then turn your arms over and raise them again. Breathe deeply and slowly through a rolled tongue. Do this for 1½ minutes.

➤ Next, move into Baby Pose. To do this, sit on your heels in a kneeling position, then relax forwards resting your torso on your thighs, your forehead on the ground and your arms by your sides, with your palms facing upwards. Relax for 4 minutes.

▲ Come back to a kneeling position, resting your hands on your thighs. Lean your torso backwards, 60 degrees to the floor – feel the stretch in your stomach. Keep your chin tucked in, your chest pushed out and hold for 1 minute. Now, lean your body forwards 60 degrees, and remain in this position for 1 minute. Next, lean backwards again, this time holding the position for 2 minutes.

◄ To finish, return to a kneeling position and cross your arms over your heart centre. Meditate to *Sangeet Kaur's Naad* – The Blessing – for 3 minutes, then sing Sangeet Kaur's ***Naad*** (see p. 160, Resources) from your heart centre for a further 7 minutes.

KRIYA FOR OPTIMUM HEALTH

Optimum Health, as taught by Yogi Bhajan on 5 October 1988

▲ Lie flat on your back with your legs straight. Bend your right knee and bring it across to the left-hand side of the body, feeling the stretch in your spine. Raise your right arm up above your head – ensure your shoulders remain on the floor at all times. Return to the starting position, then repeat the stretch with your left knee bent across your body and your left arm raised above your head. This is the Cat Stretch. Repeat the stretch for a total of 21 times on each side.

➤ Remain lying on your back with your legs straight. Raise your left leg upwards to a 90-degree angle to your torso. As you lower your left leg, raise your right leg upwards. Do this movement for 1½ minutes. This is the Alternate Leg Lifts.

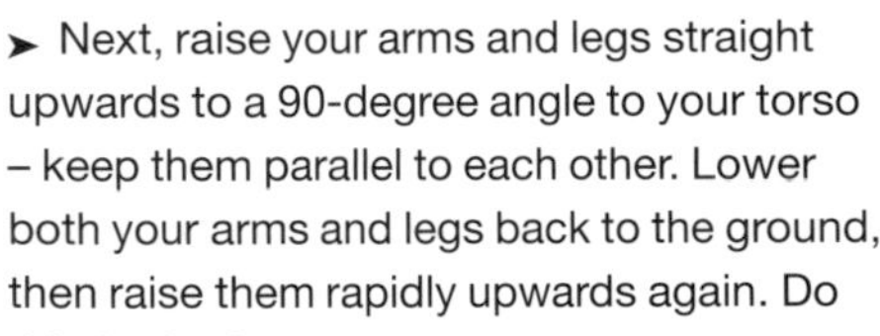

➤ Next, raise your arms and legs straight upwards to a 90-degree angle to your torso – keep them parallel to each other. Lower both your arms and legs back to the ground, then raise them rapidly upwards again. Do this for 2 minutes.

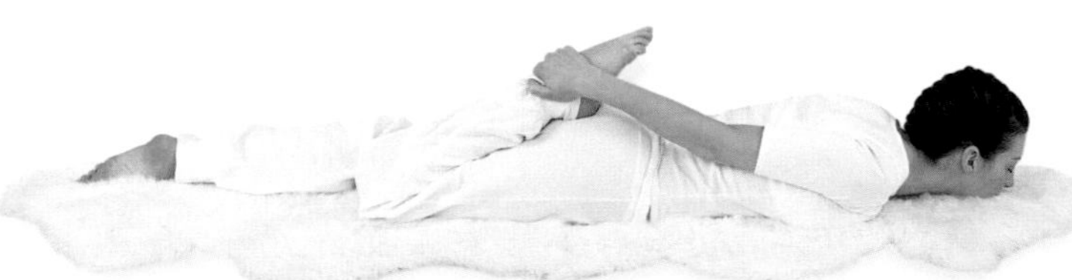

◀ Roll over and lie on your stomach. Reach for your left ankle with your left hand and draw it to your left buttock, pressing your foot against your buttock if you can. Return your ankle to the ground, then repeat with the right leg. Grab your right ankle with your right hand and bring it to your right buttock. Alternate this stretch between left and right ankle for 1 minute.

➤ Remain lying on your stomach and grab both your ankles with both your hands. Inhale and lift up your torso and thighs, holding onto your ankles. This is the Bow Pose. Rock your body backwards and forwards. Stick your tongue out of your mouth and breathe the *Breath of Fire* (see p. 30) for 1½ minutes.

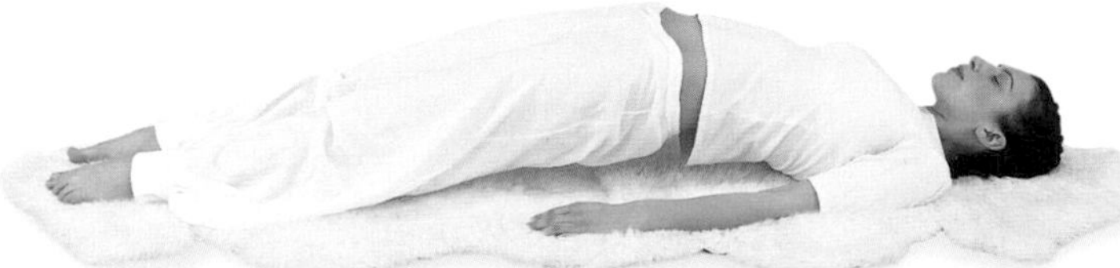

◄ Quickly roll over onto your back and tense your body. Then 'jump' your body by raising it up, down and around in a rapid motion. Do this for 2 minutes.

➤ Next, lie on your front and do the Cobra Pose (see p. 143). As you inhale, bring your torso up, and as you exhale, lower your torso back to the ground. Stick your tongue out and breathe through your mouth. Complete 54 Cobra Lifts.

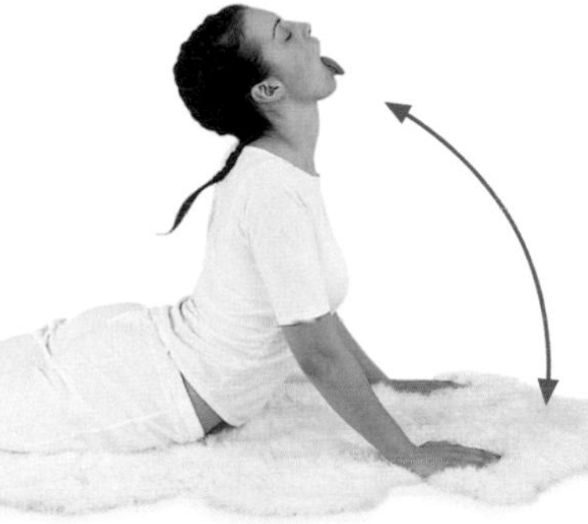

▲➤ Now lie on your back with your legs outstretched. Draw your knees to your chest and tuck your nose as close as you can to your knees. Rock backwards and forwards on your spine. Do this for 2 minutes.

➤ Next, still lying on your back, make rapid criss-cross actions with straight arms and legs. You will need to raise your legs and arms, but only as is required to clear both the ground and your body. Repeat for a total of 2 minutes.

➤ Now, grab your heels with your hands. Raise your chest off the ground, resting your weight on your shoulders, then roll your shoulders under you and lift your navel off the ground. Inhale deep into your chest, then exhale. This is the Half Wheel Pose. Do this for 6½ minutes.

Next, turn over and lie on your stomach with your arms by your sides. Continue your relaxation for 8 minutes (not shown).

➤ 'Jump' from your stomach onto your back in one movement. Lie in the Corpse position facing upwards, body and legs straight and arms by your sides with your palms facing upwards. Listen to relaxing, meditative music for 11 minutes.

Come back to your body. Rub your hands and feet together and do some Cat stretches.

➤ Meditation

Sit in Easy Pose (see p. 138). With your eyes closed, focus on the tip of your nose. Do this for 3½ minutes. Switch your focus to your third eye – the point where your eyebrows meet at the top of your nose – and meditate.

This meditation was done with Yogi Bhajan playing the gong and the song *Wha-hay Guroo, Wha-hay Guroo, Wha-hay Guroo, Wha-hay Jeeo* playing in the background.

The meditations

'Meditation is the art of breaking habits, to purify the mind and to take care of day-to-day things.' Yogi Bhajan

Much has been written about meditation, but Yogi Bhajan defined it simply as a process of cleansing the mind and not dumping a lot of thoughts into the subconscious mind. As with the practice of yoga, to meditate means to 'just be' without emptying your mind forcibly – honour your passing thoughts, whatever they may be, and let them pass. If you don't move physically, your mind will move towards stillness. This is the first stage of the meditative mind, and like the kriyas, mastery of a meditation leads to a particular state becoming reality, whether it is improved health or emotional balance.

When meditating, make sure you sit comfortably with your back straight; cover your head and body with a shawl or a blanket. As with the kriyas, keep your eyes closed unless directed otherwise.

BOOST YOUR IMMUNE SYSTEM

Boost your immune system, as taught by Yogi Bhajan on 31 January 1996

◄ Sit in Easy Pose (see p. 138). Raise your chest up and out, and tuck your chin down towards the centre of your collarbone – keep your head level and facing forwards in a neutral position, and your neck relaxed. Stick your tongue out, curving it down towards the ground as far as it can go. Breathe in and out through your mouth. Pant hard, using your diaphragm to expel the air. This is known as the *Dog Breath*. Pant for 3–5 minutes.

To finish, inhale and hold your breath for 15 seconds. Press your tongue firmly against the upper palate of your mouth. Exhale. Complete this finishing sequence for a total of 3 times.

SELF-HEALING

Self-healing (originally called a set), as taught by Yogi Bhajan on 11 December 1985

To maximise the benefit of this self-healing meditation, originally called a yoga set, follow this recommended routine each morning for 90 days: for breakfast only eat the fruit you used when doing this meditation, and only drink Yogi Tea (with some milk, if you like, but no honey). Don't eat anything else until 12 noon.

◄ For this meditation you will need either an apple or a banana. You may also want to play relaxing, meditative music to add strength to your meditation.

Sit in Easy Pose (see p. 138). If you are a man, rest the fruit in your right hand, and if you are a woman, rest it in your left hand. Cover the fruit gently by holding your other hand 5–10 cm (4–6 in) above the fruit.

Extend both your hands out in front of you. It is very important to keep your elbows straight, each hand level with the arm, and the fruit directly in front of you. Maintain this position throughout the meditation.

Close your eyes and connect with your navel centre. Project the energy that is in your navel centre to the fruit – with your hand above it, you are blessing the fruit. Remain in this position for 9 minutes, focusing on creating the energetic link between your navel centre and the fruit.

► After 9 minutes, take the piece of fruit in both your hands and draw it to your navel so that it is touching your body. Hold this position, breathing as long and deeply as you can, for 2 minutes.

Still maintaining the same position, now introduce holding your breath in and out of your body, to give a conscious rhythm to the breath. Do this by inhaling as deeply as you can, then hold your breath in for as long as you can. Next, exhale as deeply as you can, holding your breath out for as long as you can. Do this for 7 minutes.

To finish, inhale and draw the fruit in tighter against your navel. Press your tongue hard against your upper palate and exhale.

After the meditation eat the fruit consciously – chew slowly and thoroughly, and put your mind to the many blessings that you are taking into your body through this fruit.

RAA MAA DAA SAA SAA SAY SO HUNG HEALING MEDITATION

Healing with the Siri Gaitri mantra (*Raa Maa Daa Saa Saa Say So Hung*), as taught by Yogi Bhajan on 20 December 1999

Play the *Siri Gaitra* mantra on a CD or tape during this meditation, and either chant the mantra out loud or meditate silently. The recommended version is Gurnam's *RaMaDaSa Healing Sounds*.

Yogi Bhajan said about this meditation, 'It is one to practise for the rest of your life. It is a simple exercise that can give you the power to heal.'

◂ Sit in Easy Pose (see p. 138) with your left hand resting on your navel point. Raise your right hand, bend your elbow and face your palm forwards.

◂ The arm movement of this kriya is to progressively move your right hand forwards in time with the mantra. On the first syllable *Raa*, begin to extend your right hand out in front of you.

◂ Your arm should be fully extended by the time the syllable *Hung* is completed.

At the end of the process, move your arm back to the starting position with your right arm bent by your side. Begin to extend your arm again on the next *Raa*.

Your arm movement should be smooth, graceful and in time with the mantra. Move it as if you are giving a blessing.

Start by doing this meditation for 11 minutes, building up to 31 minutes, then 2½ hours.

CONQUER INNER ANGER AND BURN IT OUT

Conquer inner anger and burn it out, as taught by Yogi Bhajan on 8 March 1999

This meditation will help you to change your life. It should be done either in the morning or in the evening for 11 minutes each day and for 40 days.

▲ Sit in Easy Pose (see p. 138), then close your eyes and concentrate on your spine, which should be straight. Stretch your arms out to your sides, keeping them level with your shoulders and straight. Point your index finger on each hand upwards – these also should be straight and very stiff. Use your thumb to hold down the other fingers.

Roll your tongue and inhale. Suck the air into your body through your rolled tongue, then exhale through your nose. This is the Cooling, or Sitali, Breath. Do this breathing for 11 minutes.

To finish, inhale deeply and hold your breath for 10 seconds. As you hold your breath, stretch your arms away from your body as far as you can, feeling a strong pull. Exhale, and repeat this process of holding your breath and stretching your arms twice more.

The mantras

AS REFERENCED THROUGHOUT THE KUNDALINI YOGA COOKBOOK.

Adi mantra
Ong Namo Guroo Dayv Namo.

Adi Shakti mantra
Adi Shakti, Adi Shakti, Adi Shakti, Namo Namo,
Sarab Shakti, Sarab Shakti, Sarab Shakti, Namo Namo,
Prithum Bhagawati, Prithum Bhagawati, Prithum Bhagawati, Namo Namo,
Kundalini, Mata Shakti, Mata Shakti, Namo, Namo.

Ajai Alai mantra

Ajai Alai	Invincible. Indestructible.
Abhai Abai	Fearless. Everywhere.
Abhoo Ajoo	Unborn. Forever.
Anaas Akaas	Indestructible. Within everything.
Agunj Abhunj	Invincible. Indivisible.
Alukh Abhukh	Invisible. Free from wants.
Akaal Dyaal	Immortal. Kind.
Alayk Abhaykhe	Unimaginable. Formless.
Anaam Akaam	Unnameable. Free from desires.
Agaahaa Adhaahaa	Unfathomable. Un-damageable.
Anaatay Parmaatay	Without a master. Destroyer of all.
Ajoonee Amonee	Beyond birth and death. Beyond silence.
Na Raagay Na Rungay	More than love itself. Beyond all colours.
Na Roopay Na Raykay	Formless. Beyond chakras.
Akaramung Abharamung	Beyond karma. Beyond doubt.
Aganjay Alaykhay	Beyond battles. Unimaginable.

Chattr Chakkr Varti mantra
Chattr Chakkr Vartee, Chattr Chakkr Bhugatay,
Suyumbav Subhang Sarab Daa Sarab Jugtay,
Dukaalang Pranaasee Dayaalang Saroopay,
Sadaa Ung Sungay Abhangang Bibhootay.

Thou art pervading in all four directions,
The enjoyer in all the four directions,
Thou art self illuminated and united with all,
Destroyer of bad times, embodiment of mercy,
Thou art ever with us,
Thou art the everlasting giver of un-destroyable power.

Chotay Pad mantra
Sat Naarayan Wha-Hay Guroo,
Haree Naaraayan Sat Naam.

Sat Naraayan is the true sustainer,
Wahe Guru is indescribable wisdom,
and Sat Nam means true identity.

Ek Ong Kar Satgur Parsaad mantra
Ek Ong Kaar, Sat Gur Prasaad, Sat Gur Parsaad, Ek Ong Kaar.
There is one Creator – truth revealed through Guru's grace.

Guru mantra
Wha-hay Guroo.
I am in ecstasy when I experience the Indescribable wisdom.

Guru Gaitri mantra
Goginday Mukanday Udaaray Apaaray,
Hareeung Kareeung Nirnaamay Akaamay.
Sustainer, liberator, enlightener, infinite, destroyer, creator, nameless, desireless.

Guru Mantra of Ecstasy
Wha-hay Guroo, Wha-hay Guroo, Wha-hay Guroo, Wha-hey Jeeo.
Great beyond description is his Infinite wisdom.

Har Singh Nar Singh mantra
Har Singh Nar Singh neel Naaraayan,
Guroo Sikh Guroo Singh Har Har Gayan,
Wha-hay Guroo Wha-hay Guroo, Har Har Dhiayan,
Saakhat Nindak Dusht Mathaayan.

God the Protector takes care of the Universe. Those who live in God's consciousness and power, chant Har Har. Meditate on Wahe Guru and live in that ecstasy. Those who vibrate in God's name and relate to God all karmas are cleared.

Jap Man Sat Nam mantra
Jap Man Sut Naam, Sadaa Sut Naam.
Oh, my mind, vibrate Sat Nam, the Truth.

Laya Yoga Kundalini mantra
Ek Ong Karr Sat Naam Siree Wha-hay Guroo.
One Creator created this creation,
Truth is his name,
Great beyond description is his infinite wisdom.

Mangala Charn mantra
Ad Guray Nameh, Jugad Guray Nameh,
Sat Guray Nameh, Siri Guru Devay Nameh.

I bow to the primal Guru,
I bow to wisdom through the ages,
I bow to true wisdom,
I bow to the great, unseen wisdom.

Sat Nam mantra
Sat Naam

Sa Ta Na Ma mantra
Saa Taa Naa Maa

Siri Gaitri mantra
Raa Maa Daa Saa Say So Hung

Wah Yantee, Kaar Yantee mantra
Wah Yantee, Kaar Yantee,
Jag Doot Patee, Aadak It Waahaa,
Brahmaadeh Traysha Guroo,
It Wha-hay Guroo.

Great macroself, creative self,
All that is creative through time,
All that is the Great One,
Three aspects of God: Brahma, Vishnu, Mahesh (Shiva),
This is Wahe Guru.

References in 'bold' refer to illustrations.

Acknowledgements

Ek Ong Kar Singh and Jacqueline Koay would like to thank:

Guru Dharam Singh Khalsa, Darryl O'Keeffe, Bridget Lytton-Minor and Shakta Kaur Khalsa for lighting our Kundalini Yoga path and for a light that shines forever bright.

Camilla Davis, our editor, for her patience, support and expertise.

Ek Ong Kar Singh would like to acknowledge the love and inspiration he has received during his years of learning from:

GOD manifested in all the beautiful people he has met on planet earth.

Special gratitude to his master teacher Siri Singh Sahib Bhai Sahib Harbhajan Singh Khalsa Yogi Ji for giving him the light and the infinite awareness and knowledge.

Eliyahoo and Rachel Barber – my beloved parents for the happiness and health.

Odelia Lavie, Sarit Maor, Shai Friedman, Siri Datta, Richard McDonald and Pavllou Landragon – my spiritual brothers and sisters and soul friends for the infinite divine light.

Extra thanks to Felicitas Sopurkh Kaur, my soul friend, for the endless love, help and support she gave me during the creation of this book.

Special thanks and blessings to all of you who will read and use this book – *We Are All One God is One We Are God*.

Jacqueline Koay would like to acknowledge the support and inspiration she has received from:

Gregory Joseph Ferone for New York bliss and a sanctuary to complete this book during the unforgettable winter of 2005.

Christopher, John and Malcolm, my Three Pillars of Faith, for a lifetime of believing in me and for loving me.

Nicky, Kit, Katerina Jayne, Jack Robert and Georgina, my five beloved children, for a life worth living.

David, Harvard Boy, 'Alexander the Great' for showing me that impossible is nothing – may you continue to conquer the corporate world and to discuss Theoretical Physics passionately.

PICTURE CREDITS

Photographs on: p. 5 Copyright © 2005 Gurumustuk Khalsa – www.sikhphotos.com; p. 15 Corbis U.K. Ltd/Eye Ubiquitous/ Bennett Dean.

RESOURCES

Further information about the 'self-sensory system' as taught by Yogi Bhajan and the mantra music as specified by Yogi Bhajan.

Ancient Healing Ways
39 Shady Lane
Espanola
NM 87532, USA
Tel: 001 (505) 747 2860
Website: www.a-healing.com

3HO – Healthy, Happy, Holy Organization
6 Narayan Court
Espanola
NM 87532, USA
Tel: 001 (888) 346 2420
Website: www.3ho.org